Imagine that you a have a very limited under

unable to express your feelings. The people ar

Imagine that you keep trying to communicate i

on speaking to you. You don't make a fuss so they sit you in a chair in the lounge

all day, every day and they think you are happy to sit there because you don't

make a fuss. Imagine that you try a different way of communicating and then they

say you are too challenging to take out. So now you sit in your chair in the lounge

all day, every day."

Reference: Total Communication Film 2009

What's The Message

Copyright © 2018 What's the Message?

Dementia

www.whatsthemessage.co.uk

ISBN-9781793353566

Challenging behaviour and Dementia
About this book

Why did we write this book?

We travel all over the UK and overseas training staff and carers how to support people who are presenting behaviours that challenge. During this time, we have worked with some very experienced, passionate and dedicated people.

In a workplace, there is support from those around you and often from partner agencies. Sometimes, as a carer, it can feel overwhelming or daunting to know where to go for more information. If we are to adopt a consistent approach to behaviours that are challenging, then everyone who has day-to-day input with the person should be involved in supporting that change. This book has tools, templates and tips to help bring this consistency and help to understand why the person is challenging in the first place.

We hope you find that this book is not pumped full of clinical buzz words. Any 'jargon' we need to (which is sometimes unavoidable) is explained so that the content will be easy to understand and should be accessible. Having said that, we have mainly used our own work experience to compile this book so it is written by those who have genuine 'hands-on' experience and an operational background in health and social care.

We have structured this book in three sections:

Section One: What we should know about behaviours that challenge. This section helps to provide the background to what we mean by "challenging behaviour". It is a term often used when people display behaviours that are problematic to others. But what is the behaviour all about – in other words, *what's the message?*

Section Two: Positive Behaviour Support – The planning. Here we look at some tools and templates we can use to capture information about the message behind the behaviour. Once we have this information, we can then produce what is known as a Positive Behaviour Support (PBS) Plan. This Plan is then used to communicate the relevant information (very much like an action plan) to those people who have day-to-day involvement with the person.

If we are going to be effective at supporting a person who is deemed to be challenging, then we need to engage as many people as possible who already have contact with the person.

If one person is approaching behaviours in one way but others use a different approach, then this leads to inconsistency which will create confusion for the person and therefore make the behaviour worse. A Positive Behaviour Support Plan will address this and provide the consistency required.

Section Three: Positive Behaviour Support – The Strategies. In this final section we will explore some of the techniques (sometimes also known as *strategies or interventions)* that we can put into place. An intervention is: *involving oneself in a situation so as to alter or hinder an action or development (online dictionary).*

The agreed strategy can then be recorded on the Positive Behaviour Support Plan and will have a main focus on **"prevention strategies".**

This terms simply means things you can do to meet the need of the person before any challenging behaviours occur. The main purpose of these strategies, therefore, are to 'prevent' or reduce the behaviour that is challenging. We will give you a number of examples of how we have used these strategies in our professional life which will help you understand how the theory is put into practice.

However, with this in mind, we also recognise that there may be occasions when we are not able to prevent behaviours or trigger-events, and anxiety or challenging behaviour can escalate and occasionally lead to dangerous situations for all. We have therefore included **calming or de-escalation strategies** and, ultimately, **emergency strategies** for situations such as these.

In other words, the diagram on this page illustrates each section of the book:

Cog1: What's the behaviour? – Section 1: Background information to challenging behaviour

Cog 2: What's the message? – Section 2: Tools and templates to help us establish the Message behind the person's behaviour. This cog is often the one that is missing but is so important. We often find that most PBS plans start with identifying the behaviours (cog 1) and then jump straight to what can be done (cog 3). The problem with this approach is that the techniques or strategies that we are then using are not necessarily the right ones and can, in some cases, make matters worse!

Cog 3: What can be done? – Section 3: The techniques we can use, once we establish why the person is behaving the way they are.

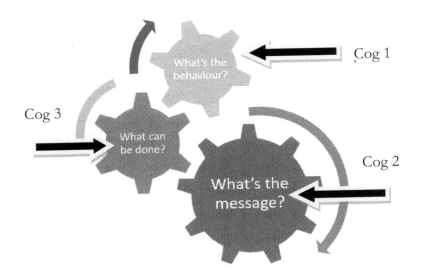

The whole focus of this book is therefore around simplicity and teaching how to support the person to use alternative ways to communicate their needs – without the use of challenging behaviour, and also what we need to think about with our own approaches and behaviour. In other words, whether we need to make a change too!

What's The Message

Final message about this book

Message Board

In this book we will be using the term 'Dementia' to describe a group of symptoms that occur when parts of the brain stop working properly. There are around 200 different types of Dementia with Alzheimer's disease being the most common form. According to the Alzheimer's Association, it is estimated that between 60 and 80 per cent of cases of Dementia are caused by this disease. It is also worth noting that is also possible to have more than one Dementia type at a time and this is commonly known as a 'mixed Dementia'.

We have included a Glossary of Terms section on page 201 which will provide some basic information on the most common forms of Dementia and a reminder about some of the terms that have been used in this book.

More detailed information about individual types of Dementia can be sought through your GP or medical professional. The message is that our book is not designed to replace any advice given by doctors, nurses or other clinical professionals.

Contents

Prologue

Before we get stuck into the contents of the book, we just want to
share a story with you ......

*Derek has been a resident in a local social care home for around 6 months. He
was referred to the home when his wife passed away suddenly. Derek has a son
who lives overseas. His brother passed away several years ago. He has no other
family members that we know of. For the first couple of weeks Derek seemed to
settle in well at the home and appeared to enjoy spending time with staff.*

*After this time, Derek starting to enter other people's bedrooms and would often
become angry and shout at other residents. This could happen in the day and
during the night. This was becoming upsetting for other residents who would, on
occasions, shout back at Derek. Derek has since started to become withdrawn.*

*Derek then started to climb on window ledges and rattle window latches. Staff
would ask Derek to come down off the ledges as they were fearful that he was
going to hurt himself. Staff tried to prevent Derek from going toward the windows,
but these actions just seemed to make matters worse.*

*The situation began to deteriorate rapidly with Derek then attempting to leave the
building where there is a busy road. Derek would rattle the doors and bang on the
glass partition. He would not leave the door and, despite attempts from staff,
would regularly go back to the exit throughout the day.*

*Derek has now started to hit out at staff when they approach him and becomes
very upset when staff attempt to intervene.*

This behaviour was now causing the family members of other residents to complain to the staff at the home. The staff were also worried about the risks and whether they were able to meet Derek's needs. Consideration was being given to Derek being moved to another home.

Details on 'the message' underpinning Derek's behaviours, and how we supported him, can be found at the back of the book. But…
before you jump to the end, keep this story in mind as we progress through the book and work through what you would do to support Derek.

Section One

What we should know about behaviours that challenge

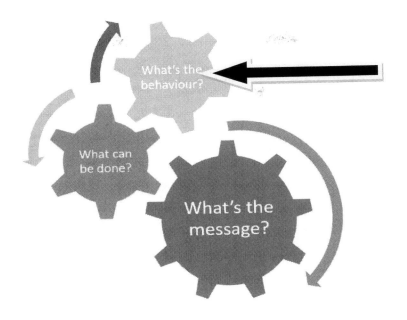

In this section we will mainly be focussing on the first of the 3 cogs in the diagram above – **What's the Behaviour?**

Chapter One
Understanding behaviours
that challenge

1. Our human needs

It is important to remember that we all have **needs and wants,** regardless of any diagnosis.

In fact, in 1943 in a paper entitled "A Theory of Human Motivation", psychologist Abraham Maslow theorised that we have what he called "layers" of needs. Maslow states that each layer of need supports the next layer within a 'hierarchy' which is typically displayed as a pyramid (see below). Maslow stated that, as a person satisfies one level of needs and stops worrying about it, the next level of needs becomes important to them.

To work through these levels, imagine that you have been stranded on a desert island.

Level 1: Food, water and basic needs. What is the most important thing you will need to survive? Food? Water? Absolutely, these are our basic needs. Once you have satisfied these needs on your desert island (collected enough coconuts to keep you going) then you may now be able to start thinking about your next level of need.

Level 2: Safety and security. With strange noises around you and night-time falling on the island, you would now probably start to think about your own safety. How secure are you? Do you need shelter? How will you keep warm? This is your Level 2 needs. This level can also include financial security along with health and emotional wellbeing. So, you build yourself a small hut out of branches and foliage and make a fire (with the box of matches you conveniently kept with you!). And… all is well. Or is it?

Level 3: Social interaction. Weeks go by and you haven't seen, or spoken to, a single person so you may start to crave social interaction with others? To satisfy this level of need, you might seek out friendship, romantic love, intimacy of sex or to be with groups of people who share common interests (for example, politics, religion, art or culture). So, you find another person on the island but….days turn into weeks, and ….

Level 4: Self-esteem. You are both bored! This level is now about having a sense of purpose and feeling a sense of worth or belonging. It may also be a need to feel valued and respected by others. This may motivate you to make money, pursue higher education or excel at a certain skill. On your desert island, this might be hunting and gathering or having a routine and job to do. In other words, a reason to 'get out of bed' in the morning. This level affects your self-esteem and is so important for your well-being and motivation.

Level 5: Personal goals. Finally, you will now be looking towards your personal goal to reach your full potential as a human being. This goal will vary through life. Interestingly Maslow suggests that less than 10 percent of people actually achieve full 'self-actualisation'. On your desert island this might be to build a raft and sail home and make a film about your experience (or maybe this has been done already with Tom Hanks in the film Castaway. If you do watch this film then look out for Wilson. Our advice to you is to have a box of tissues nearby)!

These levels of need keep us motivated in our daily lives. If our needs are taken away from us, even at a basic level, then this will have a negative impact on our quality of life which, in turn, this could mean we use challenging behaviour to get our needs met.

Reflect on this for a while in relation to the person you are supporting. Even with all of our best intentions to maintain people's needs, how many levels of needs are now truly missing from their life? Do they cook and eat the food they were used to? Do they feel safe and secure both in their own thoughts and environment? Has there been a significant change to their social life and do their daily activities reflect their interests? Do they still have a sense of purpose, job function and personal goals to achieve?

The honest answer to these questions, at this point, is probably no to all, or even most needs.

So, the question for us now is how can we ensure these needs and the life history of the person are known to everyone who is in contact with them and how can these needs remain intact for the person in some way?

In summary, this theory is not unique to a person's diagnosis. We all have needs and wants. If we are unable to communicate them to others then we may resort to challenging behaviour to get them fulfilled.

2. Types of challenging behaviour

There is no hard and fast rule on what is deemed as 'challenging behaviour'. It is important to recognise that what one person might find challenging, another might not. Spitting, for instance, would you find that challenging? Screaming, shouting or swearing? Does it matter where you are? Who you are with? Or even what mood you are in? What do you think?

Personally, in our work life, we are generally more tolerant to screaming and swearing. However, if we had a difficult journey into work, got cut up in traffic, dropped work files when getting out of the car (on a rainy day surrounded by puddles) and then tripped on the seat belt that was hanging out of the car then it is highly likely that our tolerance level to screaming and swearing might just be less than usual!

Or, if you are out in a restaurant, for example, with your children or family members and someone on another table started to swear in earshot, then would you find this challenging?

So, the very fact that we will all view challenging behaviour differently will mean that it is highly likely that we will respond to it differently. If everyone involved in the person's care is approaching the challenging behaviour in different ways then these inconsistent strategies will cause confusion and, in turn, possibly create further challenging behaviours.

3. Defining challenging behaviour

All behaviours serve some purpose or function for the individual; they are a means by which an individual can satisfy, or attempt to satisfy, a need, want or drive. They are, therefore, always 'reasonable, rational and understandable' (Mansell et al 1987)

If we are documenting challenging behaviours then we need to be clear about how we describe the actual behaviours that are concerning us. Often support plans describe behaviours with vague statements. For example: "aggressive", "violent", "intimidating". From these words, would you know exactly what the behaviours will look or feel like? No, not unless you were there to witness it.

To offer a better description, we need to be more specific, for example, "will hit others during personal care", "will pull own and other people's hair", "will scratch own face". The description of behaviour can also describe a) the intensity, for example "leaves a red mark" or "can cause bruising", b) the frequency (the amount of time the behaviour occurs) and c) the duration (the length of time the behaviour occurs). By using this more specific type of recording, we can be clear about the behaviours of concern that we need to address and that others involved in the person's care need to be aware of.

Have a go. Using the table overleaf, see if you can distinguish between behaviours that are vague and the behaviours that have a clear description.

Behaviour description exercise:

Drunk	Throws objects at staff
Slams doors	Aggression
Hits leg causing bruising	Physical
Repetitive questions about home	Makes sexist comments to others
Threatening	Gets angry
Emotional	Anxious
Screams and shouts at others	Frustrated
Shouts at own reflection in glass or mirror	Verbal

Turn to page 193 for the answers.

Now we are clear about the description of the behaviour of concern - kicking, scratching, biting - what are your thoughts on this statement? Are any of these behaviours reasonable or understandable?

Maybe not to us? However, to the person carrying out the behaviour they are! Let's think about this. Another reminder here: If the only way a person can get their need met is to use behaviour – challenging, problematic or however we describe it – then why wouldn't they? Would you?

We often hear the term 'Challenging Behaviour'. Here's one definition generally cited by Eric Emerson:

> "*culturally abnormal behaviour(s) of such* **intensity, frequency or duration** *that the physical safety of the person, or others, is placed in serious jeopardy, or behaviour which is likely to seriously limit or deny access to the use of ordinary community facilities*".

Challenging behaviour is, in essence, communicating a message or an expression of a set of problems. It is important that we recognise that challenging behaviour is not a diagnosis in its own right.

Causes of challenging behaviour may be as a direct result of changes in the person's brain or be caused by general health problems such as a urinary tract infection (UTI). It can also relate to many other reasons such as a negative reaction to the environment or a way to interact with others.

Some behaviours are displayed in order to express how we feel – they are expressions of our emotions. A flood of emotions into our body will impact on how we behave. Sometimes the flood is so intense that we struggle to control our behaviours and they then become challenging to others.

Some behaviours can occur at certain times of the day. 'Sundowning' is often a term heard in relation to Dementia. This means that the person is observed as being more agitated, irritable or challenging later in the afternoon or in the evening. There are many suggestions for this. One theory relates to damage to the brain that produces melatonin which regulates sleep and wake patterns. Disruption to melatonin could therefore cause sleep problems and a knock-on effect to this can be irritability. Another common theory is that the person might be tired or have lower energy levels as the day progresses. The opposite is also considered in that the person might be bored as they had previously been used to doing household jobs such as cooking or cleaning later in the day. Another suggestion could even be due to the day becoming darker and vision becoming poorer.

As we can see, behaviour can serve more than one function and, as such, more than one message (Miltenberger 2008). For example, a person may self-harm by scratching their face due to frustration or fear or to block out the trauma of a past memory. They may also self-harm by scratching their face because they have the need for interaction from others. Here we have the same behaviour (scratching their face) but used in different environments for different messages.

As humans, throughout our lives, we will all display behaviours that are deemed as challenging to others. It is really important we remember this and recognise that challenging behaviour is not something that is just reserved for the people we support or seen as a 'diagnosis'. Behaviours are meaningful and serve a purpose. They are about meeting a person's needs and wants. We all learn how to get these needs met and what behaviour we need to use in order to do so

So, what we are saying is that people do not get 'cured' of their behaviours – behind all behaviours lies a message – we just need to tap into what that message is. Once we understand this then we are better placed to develop support that is truly person-centred.

In this next section, we will now focus on the second of our cogs – what's the message?

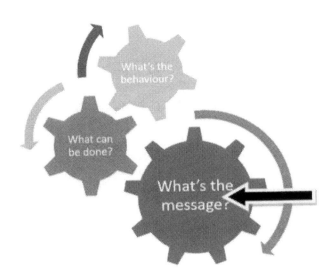

4. Challenging behaviour – what's the message?

As previously stated, the reasons why people challenge vary a lot and we are going to explore these throughout this book. Behaviour that a person engages in repeatedly will typically serve some kind of purpose or *function* for them (O'Neill, et al, 1997). When we say 'function' of behaviour we basically mean 'why – what's the message?'. Also note that we have used the word 'repeatedly' in this statement because we all engage in some type of behaviour but, unless that behaviour serves some purpose/function for a person, then it wouldn't typically continue to occur.

So, behaviours that are repeated will have a meaning and a message.

Often, the need that the person wants to have met is perfectly reasonable (e.g. they may want your attention, or need a drink or want to stop an activity or need to leave a room). However, the way they are telling us their need is through their challenging behaviour either because they have learnt to do this or there is simply no other way.

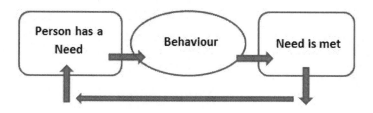

Let's look at this diagram further to help explain what we mean. So, from left to right:

A person has a need (we all have them – remember Maslow's Hierarchy of Need). The person then uses challenging behaviour to communicate that need and, in response to their behaviour, their need met – in other words, the behaviour has worked for them. So, what are they likely to do the next time they have this need? Repeat the behaviour. This cycle now becomes re-enforced as a learnt behaviour which will often repeat itself and we have to ask ourselves – if this is the only way that the person can get their need met – why wouldn't they?

A more typical example for us to use to explain this cycle can be a young child in a sweet shop. The child wants sweets (their need) and is standing right next to a vast range of goodies near the checkout. If the child screams, shouts or even throws themselves on the floor in protest (the behaviour) – what do you think they are saying to you through their behaviour? In a nutshell, 'I want sweets'! So, perhaps, and to avoid the embarrassment, Mum or Dad gives the child the sweets (need met). Aaaaah, peace is restored. Now the child has learnt. If I scream and shout next to the sweets, I get the sweets. Guess what will happen the next time the child is near the sweet aisle? And, hey, it works that well for them then they may even learn to use their behaviour for other things that they want.

If we can avoid reacting to the challenging behaviour in this way then we can avoid it becoming a cycle. In other words, we understand what the underlying message of the challenging behaviour and we either meet the persons need BEFORE the behaviour occurs or put alternative strategies in place so that the person does not need to use challenging behaviour at all in order to get their needs met.

Now for the good news…. When we consider 'the message' behind a person's behaviours, there are only 4:

- Tangible

- Escape or Avoidance

- Social Interaction

- Sensory

Let's explore this now in more detail….

We feel that an iceberg is an appropriate image to describe this next piece of theory. This is because we can all see the tip of the iceberg (which represents the person and the challenging behaviours). This is the obvious bit; the kicking, biting, crying, scratching etc. But, what about the parts of the iceberg which are below the surface that we can't see? These are the underlying reason/s for the behaviours (the message)?

To simplify this further, we are going to put these messages or functions into four groups.

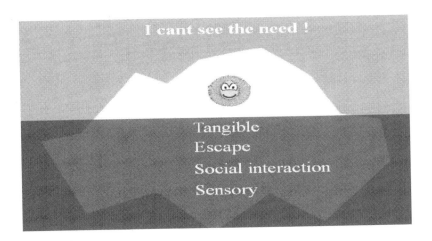

There are four types of 'message' that people may be trying to communicate through their behaviour:

a) Message 1: *Tangible*

Tangible items are anything that we can feel or touch and may include things such as sweets, drinks, a walking frame, money, the toilet, clothes, drugs or alcohol.

Sometimes, the object may be known as 'objects of reassurance'. People may become attached to certain objects (or part of objects) such as dolls, blankets, pictures or even bottle tops, coins or stones and keep them close for reassurance. These are 'security objects' and something that the person is familiar with.

It is really important to make sure everyone involved with the person understands this. We can then avoid triggering behaviours because someone, inadvertently, removes the object.

Challenging behaviour can therefore be displayed in order to gain access to items that are real to the touch and can typically occur when the person has to share, stop using or wait for the item. It may be that they are unable to understand how to gain access to the item. So, a person who is confused and is finding difficulty communicating their tangible need may try to take the item themselves — a drink, for example.... but from a stranger's cup! This might now be regarded as challenging behaviour.

It may also be that the person is unable to recall where they put an item so may become frustrated and use challenging behaviour or accuse others of theft.

Harry regularly asks about his finances and worries about his bank balance. Staff explain to Harry that he has a bank card and that he can use his chip and pin at the cash machine later in the day to access his balance and get a mini statement. This does not reassure Harry and he says that he wants to go to the bank straight away and check that his money hasn't been stolen. Unfortunately, the bank is 20 minutes away from the home by car and Harry is too upset to travel at this stage. Harry is also hiding his money in a 'secret place' but has forgotten where this is. Harry starts to shout and swear at the staff and accuses them of stealing his money. He then accuses other residents and becomes very upset This scenario is now becoming more regular throughout the day.

In this scenario, Harry wants his money (tangible) and is using challenging behaviour in an attempt to get it. Harry does not recognise what the staff are saying with terms such as 'chip and pin' and 'cash machine'. A better strategy would be to use a replica bank book (with a style that he would be familiar with) with the bank balance shown. Harry would be more likely to recognise and understand this.

It is also worth considering the fact that people with Dementia may hide or hoard tangible items in an attempt to control the situation around them. The person may be experiencing paranoia or intrusive thoughts, for example, and feel that items will be stolen from them.

Of course, when not justified, accusations of theft can be very upsetting for all those around the person but we should not always dismiss them as they may be valid.

However, if they are found not to be, then we should try to avoid taking these comments personally. The accusations may also be a 'flashback' to past experiences and the memories attached to this and the person may be confused between past and present.

If this is the case then correcting the person can often cause more upset as these emotions are 100 per cent valid and real for the person at that time.

Frustration will then occur when the person forgets where they have put the hidden items so, as a result of this, the person may challenge others to gain their tangible need. There are a few things that we can do to help here. Maybe the use of a safe place or 'hoarding box' can be used. This can be stored away and the person reminded that they can have their items placed there. It may help to have the box resemble an actual safe in some way or a storage box that the person is familiar with. If you know where the safe place is then you are in a better position to redirect them to this.

For other smaller items such as door keys, then maybe a locator device (often referred to as 'assistive technology) could be used to track the items. Or what about keeping spares of the items that are 'lost' or replacing important documents with something that resembles the item (a replica item)?

If the person is storing or hiding food or perishable items then this can lead to health issues or even some unsavoury smells! In which case we need to consider if the person is hungry throughout the day. Do they need regular snacks instead of meals and has there been a review of their dietary requirements? Maybe a referral to a dietician could help?

In summary, 'tangible' is a physical item which is real to the touch. A person therefore challenges in order to gain access to the item..

b) Message 2: *Escape or Avoidance.*

Behaviours are displayed in order to escape or avoid an activity, situation, feelings such as pain, setting/environmental condition and even a person.

We find that a high percentage of people find the noise levels and crowded environment within a residential or public setting difficult to cope with. Another difficulty can be the constant interaction with 'strangers' (whether this be medical professionals, support staff or even family members).

All of this can be extremely difficult for the person to cope with and, as a result, may lead to challenging behaviour in order to escape or avoid the situation.

In order to try and see things from the other person's perspective, and recognise how many people they interact with, try drawing a 'social map'. Do this by taking a sheet of paper, putting the name of the person in the middle and then map out all the people who are involved in that person's life (including the type of relationship the person has with them). Once you have completed this, you will start to see how many other people this person has to interact with – all (or part) of which may be a stressful experience! You can also carry out a similar exercise with the different environments the person accesses.

As a result of emotions relating to escape or avoidance, such as the fear of insecurity and anxiety of feeling unsafe, some people may also resort to what is known as 'trailing and checking' behaviour. This means that the person might start to constantly follow the carer or support worker in order to check that they are still in the immediate area.

Trailing and checking may also be related to the fact that a close relative or spouse has since died or no longer visits or the person is confused about their home setting.

In cases such as this, it is important to address the underlying emotion. Confronting the person with the truth of the situation may not help and may, in fact, escalate emotions. Telling the person that their husband died last year, for example, might mean that the person will grieve all over again. This type of strategy is called 'correction' and is something that is rarely used.

'Validating' the person's feelings may be a better approach in cases such as this or a distraction such as asking them to talk about the person they have mentioned, for example: 'I can see you're upset. Tell me about …....'. It is also worth noting that if a person is asking for home then by validating that they are safe and OK and creating an environment where they will feel this way will significantly help. Asking for home may be an indicator of insecurity as we all would like to think of 'home' as our safe haven.

In summary, challenging behaviour, in relation to escape or avoidance, is often underpinned by a range of experiences which lead to the person feeling insecure, fearful, frustrated or humiliated. It may even be due to pain or discomfort. In the words of the well-known TV programme…. escape or avoidance is communicating *Get me out of here*!

c) Message 3: *Social Interaction*

The person displays a behaviour in order to gain another person's attention.

This is the need that we often hear other people say 'they're doing it as attention seeking'. Well, yes, they are and that is a valid need. We have already learnt, with Maslow, that we all have the need for social interaction, a sense of community and to be with others. Some people may have the need for more social interaction than others and this may be seen as intrusive or constantly demanding of others' time and attention.

Margaret will sit at the dining table, laugh and throw her fork on to the floor. Staff will respond by picking it up and replacing the cutlery, asking Margaret not to throw it again. Margaret will, again, laugh and say 'of course not'. Guess what… Margaret will throw the fork again..

Margaret is getting the interaction from staff through her problematic behaviour. In cases such as this it might be worth considering a technique called *planned ignoring*. We look at this further in Section Three.

d) Message 4: *Sensory*.

Behaviours are displayed in order to satisfy a sensory feeling.

When staff attempt to assist Roger with showering, he masturbates. Some staff use humour with Roger and just tell him to 'put it away, we have seen it all before'. Other staff find his behaviour very offensive and get upset with Roger. In fact, they are quite stern with Roger and have, more recently, stated that they no longer wish to support him as his behaviour is too challenging for them. Inconsistency between staff's approaches to Roger's behaviour is now causing confusion for Roger and this behaviour is becoming more frequent.

Note: Some people with Dementia lose their inhibitions and may say things to others that is totally out of character and deemed, by society, as rude or embarrassing. What is important here is to remember that correcting the person or arguing with them will only escalate matters. The person is not doing this on purpose. In this example, for Roger, he is merely enjoying the stimulation! We need to consider how we can manage our responses here and maintain the dignity and respect for Roger.

To summarise, with the theory of the four groups of messages, or functions, in mind, now consider this scenario:

John is sitting in the living room with his wife and their dog, Lily. A white van pulls onto the drive outside the house and, at the same time, John starts to shout at the window.

Why does John exhibit this behaviour? What is the message? Tangible, Escape, Social Interaction or Sensory?

The fact is it could be any one (or more) of the four listed.

It could be a **Tangible** message, perhaps because John thinks it is a delivery van?

It could also be to **Escape** the person that just arrived in the van? John maybe doesn't like the person or has had a bad experience, in the past, with white vans!

It could be **Social Interaction** – John may be bored in the house and is excited by the thought of visitors.

It could even be **Sensory** – he may really like the feel of grooves on the tyres of the delivery van and the ridges and sparkle of the wheel trims.

So, how can we decide which **message** is relevant? We will show you a variety of tools and templates in Section Two of this book which will help you establish this.

Before we move on to that part of the book, we must have a bit more background information on challenging behaviour.

In the next chapter we will explore what happens when behaviours are triggered and escalated (the Crisis Cycle coming up next).

There are some key things we need to know about how our emotions impact on what we do. Once again, this is not just reserved for people with a diagnosis of Dementia. This is for all of us!

Chapter Two

Crisis Cycle

Kaplan and Wheeler 1983

If you keep the information in this Chapter at the back of your mind then this will help you understand what is happening to you (and others) as we creep up from a calm state, to an agitated one, to full-blown crisis. Before we start, however, consider the following scenario and what action you would be likely to take?

You are supporting a person who has just punched their relative and shouted 'all of you, go away'. He has now left the room in the direction of his bedroom. What would you do?

a) Follow him and ask him to come back and say sorry to the other person and discuss what happened

b) Leave him well alone.

c) Go to check he is OK from a distance, check the other person is OK and, when satisfied all is well, monitor from a distance.

d) Go to check he is OK and attempt to calm the situation.

What would you do and why? a, b, c, or d?

After you have considered your response to this question, now think about the best time to discuss what has just happened with the person?

Would it be best to:

a)   Speak to the person immediately while the incident is fresh in their mind?

b)   Wait for about 30 minutes and then discuss it?

c)   Wait for about 90 minutes and then discuss it

d)   Don't discuss it. The situation has happened and so it is best to just leave it.

The suggested answers to these questions are at the end of the book on page 195. However, rather than skipping straight to the answers, pause and reflect on your responses and then read the whole of this chapter. As you gain more information on this subject, you may wish to review your responses to the questions.

Let's make a start with what happens when we get anxious, upset, fearful or angry – basically when we get a flood of emotions. There are 6 stages we need to consider:

1. Baseline

2. Trigger

3. Escalation

4. Crisis

5. Recovery

6. Reflection.

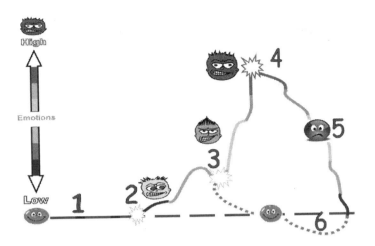

Understanding what is happening to a person as they progress through the various stages will help us to consider the different strategies that we can use which are set out in Section Three.

Stage 1: This is known as a ***Baseline*** state. We will refer to this term throughout the book so it is important to remember what this means. Hopefully, as you are reading this book right now, you are actually at baseline – feeling calm, relaxed and rational. When we are at baseline, we are able to think things through and act in a reasonable way.

As soon as we come off baseline then the 'thinking' part of our brains start to shut down. This is because our emotions are starting to flood into our brain and this reduces our quality of judgement.

This, in turn, may have an impact on how we behave. The further you escalate through the stages, the more intense the emotions will become.

Stage 2: This is called the *Trigger.* The trigger is the first move away from baseline behaviour.

There are so many reasons for trigger events. In our professional life we find that common triggers are crowded and noisy environments and also something known as *'Transitions'.* This is when someone moves from one situation to another – from activity to activity, from place to place (e.g. out of bed to shower, shower to breakfast, breakfast to putting on clothes). Transitions can be a trigger because the person might become confused and could then start to worry about what is happening next.

Sometimes staff will say that there wasn't a trigger. Remember that there is always a trigger to escalation – we just haven't seen it. This is because the trigger could be internal. In other words, something the person has smelt, an illness, pain, a past memory that's triggered an intense emotional response. In these cases, the trigger is just not visible.

We should aim, at all times, to prevent or slow down the trigger stage. However, if we miss this then the trigger stage is the time for early intervention such as calming techniques or de-escalation strategies.

Around this trigger stage, you would usually start to observe changes in behaviour - these will be displayed as 'Early Warning Signs'. Early warning signs are usually presented in 'clusters' (i.e. more than one sign).

Early warning signs could be verbal signs, such as talking loudly or mumbling or more obscure signs such as singing or manic laughing. There may be some non-verbal cues that should forewarn us. Agitation can often be recognised, for example, by restlessness, the clenching and unclenching of fists and constant movement.

Remember not to take these signs too literally, however. For example, a person rubbing their eye may have an eyelash in their eye rather than being tired or upset. Someone with crossed arms might be keeping warm or may find it comfortable to stand/sit with folded arms, rather than this being a 'defensive' pose.

It is important to know about early warning signs because when they are observed then this is the time to de-escalate or stabilise the situation. Otherwise, if the early warning signs go unnoticed, and the person's emotions/behaviours start to intensify and increase, then you will soon find out about early warning signs the hard way!

Documenting early warning signs on a support plan (and not just storing them in our heads) means that this information can be passed onto anyone who is supporting the person.

Stage 3: This is the *Escalation phase.*

The period of time between the trigger stage and the escalation stage is when we continue to use de-escalation techniques or, where possible, promote self-calming in order to help people regain control. The sooner you can use a calming strategy, the better, because the person's quality of judgement and ability to think and react rationally is starting to decline.

Generally speaking, now is not the time to place any demands on a person such as asking them to say "sorry" or to pick up something that has been thrown. In this case, "placing a demand" perhaps seems like strong words. In reality, it could be something as simple as picking up clothes from the floor or taking a coat off. This is because the rational part of the brain has either shut down or shutting down so the person is not in a reasonable state to absorb and process such information and requests.

From this point on we should also avoid ***rehashing*** what has happened. Rehashing means talking about or reliving the trigger experience or even discussing the event with another person (in earshot) or the person themselves. The emotions that were originally experienced during the event will start to come back when the person is reminded or starts to think about what happened. Emotions are intense at this point anyway so adding further emotion just adds fuel to the fire!

Stage 4: This is **Crisis** and the focus at this
stage is more about the safety and protection of yourself and others.

At this point, the brain is now completely flooded with a range of intense emotions and, therefore, the quality of judgement has now gone!

Ever heard of the Red Mist? There are various explanations for this saying. One is that in extreme anger, the whites of our eyes can become blood-shot. Another states that it is a physiological effect of a rush of blood to the head in anger or excitement which can impede our vision.

Whichever explanation we accept, the 'red mist' state is brought on by extreme stress/anger and happens when a person loses control completely and therefore loses all quality of judgement and reasoning.

If you are always reacting to challenging behaviour in this phase then nothing will change. For example, the person screams, you react with saying 'ssshh' or 'stop shouting'. The person spits and you react with 'that's not nice, don't spit'. A reactive approach will mean that it is highly likely that the same behaviours will be displayed day after day after day. Nothing will change.

There is an old saying that is very relevant for this phase - 'what we focus on will grow'. In other words, focus on the negative and that's what you will get. But on the bright side…. focus on the positive and the same theory applies. So, the message to changing behaviours is to offer or 'teach' an alternative way and different approach – for you, others and the person themselves and not get to this stage at all.

Stage 5: After Crisis we are into the **Recovery Phase.**

In the Recovery Phase, a person will start to move back to a Baseline stage and mood. Heightened emotions and adrenaline can remain in the body for an average of ninety minutes and this can even last up to a couple of days. The length of time will depend upon the intensity of emotion from the Crisis. If this is the case, then all the things we learnt about the Escalation stage needs to be considered for the Recovery stage. Watch for any signs of re-escalation, avoid placing demands on the person, use calming strategies or assist the person with self-calming and relaxation techniques.

And finally…

Stage 6: Time to think – this is the **Reflection Phase.**

This is the point when a person is in a better emotional state to be able to discuss and consider what happened because the quality of judgement and reasoning is starting to return.

Before we go onto the next chapter, can you recall we did an activity on page 37 and 38. Would you like to recap on that exercise now and see if you would like to change your answers?

If so, then flick to the back of the book and have a look at what we suggested for responses.

So why do we lose our quality of judgement? Why do we have a rush of emotions? Why do we lose our self-control and reasoning?

The answer is in our brain…. Yes, we all have one! Let me introduce the next Chapter – **the Human Brain.**

Chapter Three

The Human Brain

Let's make no mistake here, the brain is an extremely complex organ. It may only weigh around 3 pounds but it is packed with around 100 billion neurons and 100 trillion connections. This is also why there are over 200 different types of Dementia because the brain is so vast and complex with so many different areas to affect. The brain controls everything – what we think, how we feel and what we do.

The brain comprises 75 per cent water, so even the smallest amount of dehydration can have a negative impact on how our brain functions. The brain is just like the rest of our bodies, it needs looking after. That means a healthy diet, plenty of rest and sleep and to be exercised too!

Dementia occurs when different parts of the brain are impaired or no longer function due to disease or damage to the brain tissue. At first, this damage may be isolated to certain parts of the brain which means that, in the early stages, each type of Dementia will tend to have a different impact on how the person experiences the world and how they behave. In later stages, however, as the mass of tissue damage progresses throughout the brain, the symptoms across the different types of Dementia can start to appear quite similar as more parts of the brain are affected.

Until recently, research into Dementia, and the impact upon the brain, very much relied on studying the brain after the person had died. Nowadays, however, with the help of technology, these studies can take place while the person is alive, usually through brain scans, which can detect the areas of reduced activity and also where there is brain-tissue damage.

This chapter is not about giving you the advanced knowledge of a brain surgeon (although, as an aside, there are allegedly signs of brain surgery recognised as far back as the Stone age). Instead, we feel it is helpful for you to know a little bit about the brain so that you can try to better understand the Dementia more and, therefore, support the person better.

Within this chapter we are also going to look at how changes in the brain impact on changes to a person's behaviour and which areas of the brain are considered to be responsible for which skills and abilities. So, let's turn the page and make a start with the following:

- The Neocortex
- The Limbic System including the Thalamus, Amygdala and Hippocampus

1) The relationship between the Neocortex and Limbic System

Let's do our own bit of surgery now and dissect the brain by slicing it straight down the middle (not literally, of course)! In this section, we will look at the first 2 parts: Neocortex and Limbic System.

Have you ever heard the saying – "Being ruled by your heart and not your head"? In summary, this describes these parts of a neurotypical brain (i.e. without damage) that we are going to focus on in this section:

a) The Neocortex. This is the higher functioning 'head' part of this phase, (the rational, reasoned side that controls our intellect)

b) The Limbic System. This is the 'heart' and our emotional side. Let's look at each of these areas in more detail.

Imagine that the Fig. 1 represents the brain chopped in half:

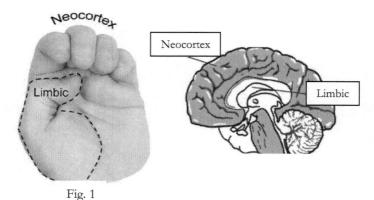

Fig. 1

All of the fingers together represent the Neocortex. Have you ever seen an old black and white movie with the eccentric looking scientist in his laboratory? In the scene you may see a brain pickled in a jar. That grey, wrinkled part is the Neocortex and, if it was rolled out, it would be about the size of a broad sheet newspaper. It is what we commonly call 'the grey matter'. The Neocortex is the *reasoning part* of the brain that helps us think straight!

However, as a person becomes stressed, anxious, fearful or angry (in fact, any type of emotional flooding), then the thinking part of the brain (Neocortex) shuts down, either slowly throughout the day or as quick as the flick of a switch. This leaves the next part – the Limbic system - in charge. In other words, being ruled by our chaotic emotions!

Introducing the **Limbic system**….. This is represented by the thumb area and is tucked inside the Neocortex. This is the 'emotional' part and does not get involved with thinking.

In a nutshell, if our brain is dominated by the Limbic (emotional) part, with no input from the Neocortex (thinking part) then we would become overwhelmed with feelings and become irrational.

If the reverse happened - all 'logical' and no 'emotional' brain - then we may appear cold, heartless, computer-like people – like Dr. Spock from Star Trek!

a) Dissecting the Limbic System

Fig 2: The Thumb represents
the Limbic System:

Within the Limbic System are:

- The Thalamus

- The Hippocampus

- The Amygdala

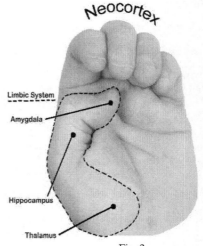

Fig. 2

b) The job of the Thalamus

If we now dissect the Limbic system further, in the neurotypical
brain, the Thalamus part is like two egg-shaped masses and is situated
at the base of the Limbic system above the brain stem (represented
on the diagram as the 'squidgy' part at the base of your thumb).

The Thalamus is the 'sub post office' of the Limbic system. In other
words, it identifies and sorts different lower level sensory information
that it receives - sight, sound, taste and touch. You may have noticed
that there is one sense left out.... more about the sense of **smell**
later (page 56).

Although the Thalamus 'sorts' information, it is not known as the 'clever' part of the brain as it has to send these sensory signals to the higher functioning parts of the brain for processing and decisions. Clearly if there is damage to the Thalamus then the sensory information may not get transferred quickly or it might go to the wrong area and confusion could result.

When the sensory information enters the Thalamus, it is never 100% certain if there is a threat to you, or not. If we can remain calm and if there is no damage to this part of the brain, then the Thalamus will send out a a quick memory check to its 'next-door neighbour', the Hippocampus (represented in Figure 2 by the middle part of the thumb).

c) The job of the Hippocampus

The Hippocampus has an unique shape, similar to that of a seahorse.

It is also the catalyst for long-term memory and the memory of objects and people (spatial memory).

In other words, for example, if you had previously visited or walked somewhere in your past then, thanks to your Hippocampus, you will successfully navigate yourself back as your Hippocampus registers where you have been – your built-in Sat Nav, so to speak!

The Hippocampus will also help to convert short-term memory into long-term memory.

It's worth noting that some types of Dementia - such as Alzheimer's disease - are linked to the Hippocampus because it is often damaged first. This makes it hard for the person to form and store new short-term memories. So, due to the damage, the person may forget tasks that they did during the day or what they have just heard or said.

However, within the earlier stages of Alzheimers, the Hippocampus is still able to recall longer-term memories, so this is why a person may recall memories from their younger years but not what they have done that day. Unfortunately, as Alzheirmer's disease spreads through the brain, additional areas will become affected meaning that longer term memories will also be lost as the brain is gradually damaged.

Another, less common forms of Alzheimers - Posterior Cortical Atrophy (PCA), for example will have other parts of the brain affected first so the damage may not be in, or even near, the Hippocampus. This means that early symptoms may not be the memory loss.

Now, combining the Thalamus and Hippocampus, consider this scenario in a neurotypical brain:

You're lying in bed and are woken by a scratching sound at your window. If you stay calm and rational, your Thalamus will receive information and post the incoming sound of the scraping to the Hippocampus (memory) and ask "excuse me, but have we ever heard this scraping sound before? And, if so, what did we do about it last time?"

The Hippocampus will do the memory check and reply "yes, don't you remember you asked your partner (the one snoring next to you) if they could cut the branch as it was getting close to the window and scraping it". At this point, both parts would engage with the Amygdala to check on a fear response – are we scared by this or not?

d) The job of the Amygdala

The Amygdala – or Amygdalae, because we have two - are almond shaped and can be found situated a few inches from either ear. The diagram below represents the full brain – the thumbs represent the Amygdala which are situated towards the back of the brain:

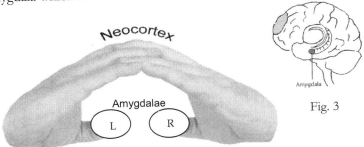

Neocortex

Amygdalae

L   R

Fig. 3

The Amygdalae are critical in regulating and processing emotions and in guiding emotion-related behaviours and is regarded as our 'emotional thermostat' - starting from a 'calm' or baseline stage and rising to 'danger' or crisis point.

An example of your Amygdala working would be if someone creeps up behind you and pops a balloon without you knowing. BANG! Your 'thermostat' immediately jumps straight to 'danger' and red alert. Once the Amygdalae are triggered, then it sends the warning signals through the brain and out via the nervous system into the adrenal glands. These glands then respond by pumping adrenaline throughout the bloodstream. This is commonly known as a 'Fight or Flight' response.

The Fight or Flight Response was originally discovered by the Harvard physiologist Walter Cannon in the early 1900's who stated that this response is hard-wired into our Limbic brains and designed to protect us from risk and harm. It is our most primitive and automatic response and originates from the early days when we were cavemen and needed to survive daily threats, such as wild animals or dinosaurs! Studies on rats where scientists removed the Amygdalae, proved the rats no longer had a fear response – not even when introduced to a rather large cat!

Today, however, we don't have to worry about a wolf (or dinosaur) coming around the corner. Instead, our Flight or Fight responses are now triggered by a more modern set of issues, such as road rage or an argument with a family member!

So, when this Fight or Flight response is activated and adrenaline released, it can cause dramatic changes to our body - blood rushes into the muscles and limbs that need extra energy and fuel for fighting or running, our breathing intensifies, our heart races faster and overall awareness within our senses intensifies. If we are in fight or flight mode, we bypass the Neocortex (thinking part) of the brain so this may cause us to behave differently and have exaggerated fears or become hyper-sensitive to things other people are saying.

With all of this information in mind, we can now think back to the scenario of the branch scratching the window in the middle of the night. The Thalamus and Hippocampus would process the basic information and pass this to the Amygdala for it to do a quick 'fear check' based on the memory and recollection of events. If the Amygdala recognises a threat then it will send a signal you to either fight (jump out of bed and run to the window) or freeze (stay in bed and hide under the duvet cover). If it recognises no threat then it will just let you relax and sleep.

The Amygdala and Hippocampus are also responsible for **phobias** as they are connected to the memories of past trauma the person (or somebody they were with) has experienced. The fear associated with the trauma experience stays jointly lodged within Hippocampus (memory) and Amygdala (emotions).

The Amygdala doesn't 'remember' the event, but it does 'remember' the emotion connected to it. If you think of the phobia as balancing scales for your memories, then negative memories are weighing down the good ones. Some people resort to hypnosis to retrain the brain to cope with the phobia. Another method is to find ways of building new 'good' memories around the phobia to redress the balance.

In summary, the Hippocampus and Amygdala are closely connected. The Hippocampus remembers the factual content whilst the Amygdala recalls the emotion attached to the facts.

In Alzheimer's disease, various studies have identified that the Amygdala is generally affected later than the Hippocampus. If there is damage to the Amygdala then this can lead to a person reacting with extreme emotions or on the flip side of this, a complete lack of emotional responses to events or people.

So…. to the sense of **smell** - we haven't forgotten it! Where does that get processed? The information our brain receives through smell is not processed through the Thalamus. It is, in fact, processed through our Olfactory Bulb which is positioned just behind the top of our nose. The sense of smell is very privileged as it has direct contact with both our Hippocampus (memory) and our Amygdala (thermostat).

So, you smell popcorn and what do you associate this with? Maybe with a childhood memory of being at the cinema? The smell of a freshly polished hall or the smell of a new book takes you back to what? Maybe school and the memories you had there - good or bad. What about the dentist? As soon as you step through the dentist door you get that all too familiar smell and your stomach immediate flips and your heart rate increases.

Remember the sense of smell has direct 'VIP connection' with memory (Hippocampus) and your emotional thermostat (Amygdala). Knowing this, we can start to think about how this might trigger a person's behaviour. We might not even realise that there is a certain smell in the air, from for example, our perfume or the smell of a certain food. Ultimately, the person might simply dislike the smell but it could also trigger memories from the past! Smell is sometimes used in therapy sessions as it can also provoke past happy memories and be calming for a person.

With some forms of Dementia, there is various studies suggesting that, because of the damage to the brain, a person's perception of smell may be lost or distorted. Therefore, we must establish, from a medical professional, whether a person's sense of smell has been damaged in any way before we begin to introduce that form of therapy into our support plans.

Our final thought for you - the next time you visit your travel agents to look at the possibility of booking your holiday in the sun, see if you notice the smell of sun tan lotion or coconuts in the shop. That smell will probably trigger all those happy memories of you sunbathing and enjoying your holiday and this is going to make it far more likely that you go ahead and book that holiday! Or the next time you are thinking of buying a house and you go for a viewing, watch out for the smell of fresh coffee and baking of home-made cakes or bread! Apparently, according to a high percentage of estate agents, this is more likely to get you to think of the house as 'home'. Clever, huh?

We can use all of this information to help us. We can use smells that the person likes or that can be calming to block out any uncontrollable smells that could lead to anxiety.

2) The 2 Hemispheres and impact on Dementia

Let's go back to our representation of the brain. The whole of the surface of the hands in the diagram (Fig. 4) makes up what is known as the 'Hemispheres.' There are 2 Hemispheres - the left and right. They are separated by a deep furrow and connected together by a bridge called the Corpus Collosum which enables the transfer of information across the two sides. Over and above this, information about what we see, think or do transfers all over the brain between 'Neurons'. These Neurons move at different speeds – the fastest being 250mph!

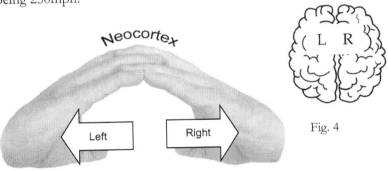

Fig. 4

The **left** Hemisphere controls the co-ordination of the right-hand side of the body. It is an overall responsibility for the logical and analytical skills such as reasoning, number skills, science, calculations and mathematics. It also controls our language (in 95% of right-handed people, the left Hemisphere is dominant for language. Even in 60-70% of left-handed people, the left Hemisphere is used for language).

Damage to all, or part of, this hemisphere will cause disruption to some or all of these processes.

The **right** Hemisphere controls the co-ordination of the left-hand side of the body. This side is responsible for creativity, artistic expression, intuition, insight, imagination and appreciation of music.

Although the two sides have different functions, they work together to complement each other. You don't just use one side of your brain at a time. In fact, it is actually a myth that we only use 10 per cent of our brain. We actually use all of it. We're even using more than 10 per cent when we are asleep!

If blood supply is cut off to one, or both, of the brain's hemispheres then this can cause damage. If the left Hemisphere is damaged then this will affect the right side of the body and vice-versa. As a result of this damage, the person may be left with physical weakness which could lead to problems with vision, speech or movement of the side of their body (opposite to the hemisphere that is affected).

A type of Dementia known as 'Vascular' follows after a major stroke, or a series of several mini-strokes over a period of time, so this will disrupt the functions of either the left or right Hemisphere (or both). As a result of the stroke, Vascular Dementia will be more likely to have more variable symptoms than other types of Dementia.

To summarise this section, let's just have a quick quiz.

Which Hemisphere do you think is being used for each of the following:

a)   Movement of the left hand

b)   Movement of the right foot

c)   Talking to a relative

d)   Doing a crossword

e)   Drawing an imaginary superhero

f)   Daydreaming

g)   Listening to a friend

Answers to this will be on page 197

3) The 4 Lobes: Frontal, Temporal, Parietal and Occipital

In the final part of this chapter we will go back to looking at the full Cortex part of the brain which includes the right and left Hemisphere. If you recall, this part of the brain is the wrinkly grey matter which is tightly packed with Neurons that transmit the information around the brain.

Over time, the brain accumulates more and more knowledge and this process creates more wrinkles. So, in essence, many researchers state that the more wrinkles in the brain, the more intelligent you are. This is because these extra wrinkles will increase the overall surface area of the brain which, in turn, leads to more brain mass and, subsequently, more, and stronger, neurons. Well, this has to be the only time we think it is great to have loads of wrinkles!

The lobes, in the wrinkly bit, are responsible for 'higher thought processes' and are divided into four, each with their own functions:

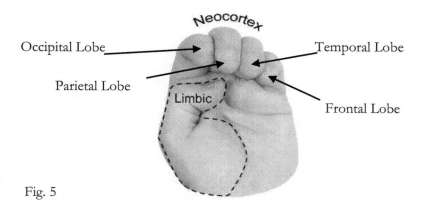

Fig. 5

The fingers now represent the 'Lobes'. Here they are again with their exact positions:

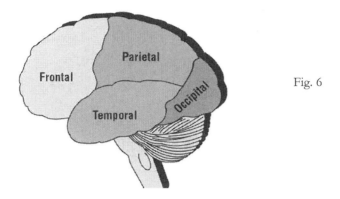

Fig. 6

Each of these lobes have a function so let's take a look at each one individually and how this relates to the diagnosis of Dementia:

a) The Frontal Lobe

This part of the brain is the largest of the Lobes and located at the front of the skull. In essence, the 'control panel' of our personality including our inhibitions and impulses. The Frontal Lobe also carries out higher mental processes such as planning, decision making, and problem solving. This is where good, or even bad, decisions are made and understanding the consequences to our actions.

The Frontal Lobe usually matures around the age of 25. No excuse for not understanding the consequences to our actions after this age then!

Damage to the Frontal Lobe can also lead to an increase in irritability, which may even include a change in mood, lead to the person becoming withdrawn, demotivated or to lack enthusiasm. In essence, the inability to regulate our behaviour.

As such, damage to the Frontal Lobe may also cause obsessive behaviours such as compulsively shaving, binge eating, folding a cloth, taking shoes on and off, touching something over and over again or even repeating words over and over again. The damage can even include a change of our personality or beliefs so a person could become obsessed with gambling, for example, when they had never done this before the damage.

Damage to this surface area will also cause disruption to a person's verbal and physical inhibitions and social tact. This means that they may undress at inappropriate times, masturbate in front of others, swear, eat non-food items or make sexual/inappropriate comments to others.

If the person has damage to this part of the brain, along with the Hippocampus, then they may also struggle with something known as 'sequential processing' which basically means processing facts and information that is in a sequence.

The inability to process sequences is caused by a dysfunction of the Frontal Lobe affecting the 'Working Memory'. Working Memory is basically a temporary storage bin for information that is needed to complete a specific task. It differs from Short Term Memory because it is the ability to not just remember information for a period of time but to use, move it around and then apply and discard it.

The average capacity for storing information is generally 7 pieces of information (plus or minus 2). So, the average highest capacity for information would be 9 and the lowest generally being 5. This is nothing new. We have been learning to store letters, numbers and sequences this way since we were children. How did you remember the alphabet? ABCDEFG….. HIJKLMNOP….. QRSTUVW… XYZ.

Think about how you remember your mobile phone number. This is usually 5 numbers followed by 2 sets of 3. The way we remember long pieces of information is to therefore 'chunk' them. We all do it our own way. But then you recite your phone number to another person and they may recall it back in a different way. Can you recognise your number when they read it back to you in their own chunk? Probably not!

If there is a working memory deficit caused by damage to the Frontal Lobe and Working Memory, then the person's ability to store and manipulate each piece of information could therefore reduce down to as little as 1 piece.

Therefore, asking someone with damage to the Frontal Lobe to switch off the television and then come over to the table or to get dressed and then go over to have a shower could overload the working memory and cause frustration, confusion or even challenging behaviour!

b) Temporal Lobe

Frontotemporal Dementia isn't just one condition. It is, in fact, several disorders that affect the Frontal and Temporal Lobes of the brain. It used to be called Pick's Disease after Arnold Pick, the physician who first discovered it. Various types of research now estimate that this type of Dementia is responsible for approximately 15% of all diagnosed cases.

One of the most significant differences between Alzheimer's disease and Frontotemporal Dementia is that Frontotemporal Dementia will often present itself between the ages of 45 and 65 whereas Alzheimer cases are often diagnosed in those over 65.

The Temporal Lobe is located at the bottom, middle part of the brain just behind the temples and close to the ears. Due to its location, the primary function of this lobe is to help us receive sensory information, in particular, the sounds and language we hear.

However, the function of the temporal lobe doesn't just stop there because the Hippocampus is also located in the Temporal Lobe. This means that this portion of the brain is also responsible for the formation of memories and linking these memories to our senses.

Ultimately, we all have different and personal memories. These memories are stored in our brains and have a direct impact on how we behave because they make up who we are today.

When considering why a person might be behaving in a certain way, it is helpful to understand a little bit about the particular memory types, and what happens when these memories are disrupted or fail.

The first type of memory is known as **'episodic'** which relates to the recollection of personal events and experiences. This type of memory is autobiographical and unique to you (and only you). This could be memories of big events such as your wedding day, passing your driving test or smaller events such as where you left your car key or what you ate for breakfast.

A memory of this type, for example attending a party, may seem the same to that of someone else's who attended but it will differ because we will have our own unique feelings, perceptions, thoughts etc of this event. These memories are yours….. and only yours!

For episodic memory to work, however, we need to retrieve, retain and action these memories (often referred to as 'encoding'). If this process does not function properly then we may forget where we put our keys or what we had for breakfast.

The second type of memory is known as **'Semantic'** and refers to facts, meanings and knowledge that we have acquired. It would include things like the names of capital cities in the world, functions of different objects such as using a knife and fork understanding different types of food.

It is episodic memory that is most affected in Alzheimer's Disease so memory for events may be a problem. This will mean that the person may be able to recognise where they are at one moment but then, seconds later, ask who you are and where they are.

c) Occipital Lobe

The Occipital Lobe is at the back of the brain. In fact, 'occipital' comes from the Latin for 'back of the head'.

It is the smallest of the lobes covering approximately 12 per cent of the total surface of the Neocortex. Whilst it is the smallest, in our daily lives, we probably rely on this the most! It's primary responsibility is to interpret what the eyes see. It will receive the visual stimuli from the eyes, process the information and then forward this to other parts of the brain for responses.

The most common form of visual impairment is damage to the eye itself. A less common one could be damage to the Occipital Lobe. This is because, whilst the healthy eye can transmit the information to the Occipital Lobe however the lobe itself cannot send what it receives to other parts of the brain to process.

Take a moment to look at an object in the distance. Within a split second, your brain has registered this, processed the shape, colour, contours of the object, the distance and size in relation to where you are and the other objects around it and then it has checked back to identify it as a whole. The Occipital Lobe is busy bouncing this information back and forth around the brain all day as it interprets what our eyes are seeing!

Damage to the Occipital Lobe may therefore mean an inability to recognise the shape and contours of such everyday objects. We can help with this by using vivid contrast colours with objects such as plates, cups, table tops or toilet seats to help distinguish between the objects. Red, navy, blue, turquoise and black are all good colours to use. For example, a red toilet seat will help to distinguish it from the rest of the toilet pan.

Such difficulties do not just stop at the inability to recognise objects. It may also mean that the person is unable to recognise faces (even those that had been previously familiar to them). This is known as 'face blindness' and is a topic that we will cover in more detail, starting on page 129

Peripheral vision can also be affected. If this is suspected then we can help here by trying to avoid approaching from the side of the person. Instead, proceed slowly and hold out open hands to enable the person to see you approaching.

Finally, damage to the Occipital Lobe can also cause visual hallucinations (which means seeing things that are not really there). The person may also experience something known as 'misperception'. This means that they may mistake objects, such as clothes hanging on a coat hanger, for a person!

Hallucinations and misperceptions can be so convincing to the person that they can cause delusions and possibly even a state of paranoia as the person may be convinced that they are being watched or they may state that something is there when it clearly isn't.

Having said all this, before we make any assumptions that a person is experiencing hallucinations or misperceptions, we should consider whether what they are perceiving is caused by other factors such as a high temperature, seizures, certain medications (or combination of), protein deposits on the brain (known as Lewy Bodies) or illness. It could also be that the person is unable to verbally communicate what they see or have mistakenly misinterpret things.

In any case, specialist visual testing should be arranged and a medical review to rule out any of these issues.

d) Parietal Lobe

This lobe is located just behind the Frontal Lobe in the top, rear part of the brain. It organises and interprets the sensory information that is sent to it from all over the body.

Shrinkage to this lobe and the Occipital Lobe would be most common in PCA (Posterior Corical Atrophy - an atypical form of Alzheimers).

Damage to this lobe will create problems with 'spacial awareness' which means difficulty in locating, judging and the co-ordination of objects within our personal space. Therefore, tasks such as stepping onto a pavement, reaching out to pick something, picking up a fragile item such as a flower or walking up steps might all prove difficult. The damage can also cause problems with processing tactile information such as pressure, touch and pain.

Damage to special awareness can increase the risk of falls or limit certain activities for daily living such as getting into the shower (which would include tasks such as negotiating the step, locating the toiletries, turning on the shower etc), getting dressed (locating the buttons, zips, picking up the clothes, placing an arm into the sleeve) and eating (putting the spoon under the plate to put the put food on or turning the spoon the other way up to pick up the food)

While we can't change how the brain processes the spatial awareness, we can arrange regular checks to see if the person's vision is functionally optimally or if glasses are required or the correct prescription.

Quick quiz: Which Lobe?

From the following statements, which Lobe do you think would be affected?

a) Sometimes he doesn't recognise me, and once he has told me to get out of his house

b) She often talks about seeing things that are not there

c) He speaks quite openly about what he thinks of other people. He used to be such a shy man.

d) He keeps talking about going to work but he hasn't worked for over 5 years now

e) She says that there are rats and snakes in her bed but there is nothing there

f) He keeps repeating the same thing over and over again

g) She can't seem to remember what she did 5 minutes ago

h) He is being really rude to people and making sexualised comments. This is just not like him

i) She just won't get out of bed and seems really low

Answers can be found on page 197

Final thought – Remember the person

Whilst we now have this basic knowledge of the brain it is crucial that we remember that challenging behaviour, or, in fact, behaviour of any kind, is not just caused by changes in the brain. There are so many other factors that play a part.

Therefore, when we look at supporting a person with Dementia, we need to consider the whole person and their social environment. This could include their life experiences, needs, wants, wishes, beliefs or values.

The person may still get enjoyment from activities that are meaningful for them. Not just activities that are available. For activities to be meaningful we need to consider the person's life history. What type of things did they enjoy doing creatively – hobbies, interests and pastimes? This could be doing anything that the person benefits from whether this is enjoyment, fulfilment or comfort.

When supporting a person with Dementia we also need to focus on what the person can do – the person's abilities, not their disabilities. The positive aspects are just as important. Remember the old saying– 'what we focus on grows'. In other words, if we focus on the negative then we get the negative, if we focus on the positive aspects then we are more likely to get just that.

Section Two

Planning for

Positive Behaviour

Support

Now that we have a general understanding of 'behaviours that challenge', we need to now look at ways to establish what the message is behind the behaviour. So, let's continue to look further into Cog 2.

Rather than making assumptions or simply guessing about the message of the person's behaviour, we should, instead, analyse or carry out some form of assessment to establish this.

This section will offer you a range of tools and templates to help you contribute towards this assessment process.

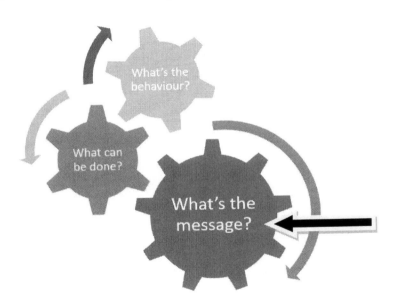

Chapter Four

Positive Behaviour Support: Planning

We've already shared a number of hints and tips throughout the first chapter – things that we need to think about for ourselves and others.

Over the next two sections we can start by planning a consistent approach to support the behaviour change and then considering some strategies that could be used.

To do this we will use what we call Positive Behaviour Support (PBS). The focus of PBS is not on 'fixing' the person and it never uses punishment as an intervention for dealing with challenging behaviour. PBS is based upon the principle of guiding someone towards a more effective and acceptable behaviour than using the challenging one or perhaps changing the environmental conditions where the challenging behaviour is more likely to happen.

What is a Positive Behaviour Support (PBS) Plan?

A PBS plan is created to record what the behaviour is about - what's the message behind the behaviour? A PBS plan also summarises what needs to be done to support or change the behaviour. It provides guidance to all those involved with the person so that everyone understands the correct strategies to be used and the reasons why.

The more people you have involved with the strategies you are implementing, then the more consistency you can build for the person.

Everyone has different values and beliefs about what is right and wrong and how behaviour 'should' be managed. This is based on their own experiences. Using a PBS plan means that you can avoid everybody 'doing their own thing' based on what they think is best or appropriate and introduce a consistent approach which is clearly understood by all those involved.

1. How to create a basic Positive Behaviour Support Plan

A PBS plan can be carried out by a behaviour specialist in collaboration with all those who are involved with the person; carers, family, support workers. It is an information gathering exercise in order to establish the 'message' behind the behaviour. You should be able to access a behaviour specialist service through the person's GP or Social Worker. You can help with this process by using a variety of tools and templates to identify what the message behind the person's behaviour might be.

The PBS Summary below is an example of what we use in our professional work.

Positive Behaviour Support Plan
Name: XXXXXXXX.

Name: Date:	Review date:
History: past hobbies, past employment, family, friends, interesting facts:	
a	

Likes:	**Dislikes:**
b	b

Diagnosis/medical Information:
c

Support strategies

Behaviours identified:
d

What's the message? tangible, escape, social interaction, sensory?
e

Triggers	**Early warning signs:**
f	g

Actions used to prevent the behaviours (70% baseline strategies):
h

Actions used to de-escalate the behaviours (20% de-escalation strategies):
i

Actions used to react to the behaviours (10% crisis strategies):
j

Working through the plan from top to bottom, this is what each section would typically contain:

a) History: This section will provide a summary of the person's history and background and will include information such as place of birth, friends, marital status, family members and friends (and the person's relationship with them), known pets. Consider their hobbies and interests, their previous work and cultural/religious beliefs and any other interesting facts about the person's life. Think about 'Maslow's Hierarchy of Needs' for this section. In other words, consider each layer of Maslow as a 'checklist' – layer 1-5: what does the person like to eat, drink, what makes them feel safe and secure, who do they interact with, what was their job function or career, goals and aspirations.

b) Likes/Dislikes: The next part is a précis of the person's likes and dislikes, what is important for and to the person. This section will also include Maslow's Hierarch of Needs' and, whilst important, is not just reserved for layer 1 (food and nutritional aspects). Think about meaningful activities that the person enjoys, favourite places and preferred times to eat, rest or for family to visit. Do they like to have a newspaper every day, watch the news, go to bed at a certain time or other routines? Do they dislike crowds and noise, having the light switched off/on at night or having other people sitting with them at mealtimes (remember, not everyone wants to sit around a table to eat)?

c) Medical information and the person's diagnosis. Some of the issues you might like to consider would be, for example, what type of Dementia? Any other conditions that are current? Is the person susceptible to urinary tract infections? In this section it can also be helpful to record how the diagnosis can manifest – you may know how it manifests but will others know? Are there any side effects that may be present through the diagnosis? Are there any side effects of medication or the combination of medication? Has there been a recent medication review?

d) Behaviours identified: Compile a list of behaviours of concern (remember to have a clear description of these), for example: will hit self in face which will cause bruising, will pull hair of self and others.

e) What's the message? Refer back to page 27 in the book about what purpose the behaviours listed above actually serve? What is the function? Tangible, escape, social interaction or sensory? A full assessment would need to be carried out to establish what function is being served by the challenging behaviour. Remember that challenging or problem behaviour happens for a reason

f) Triggers: Once again, refer to page 40 to consider what the triggers are or might be. Consider personal conditions such as what the person dislikes, e.g. crowds, noise, certain people, colours etc and then environmental conditions such as noisy areas, cold, heat, too much stimulation.

g) Early warning signs: Refer to page 40. In this section, we need to record what the physical and observable signs are that the person is becoming angry, upset, fearful, frustrated – in other words, any surge of emotions? What does it actually look like or sound like?

Early warnings signs generally come in clusters and are not usually just one sign so look closely for these (not too close though)! For example: the person will pace up and down the corridor, clenches fists or teeth, has a fixed eye contact, will look away, mumbles under breath, taps fingers or foot, folds arms and hunches forward. These are all examples of early warning signs and have a clear description. Make sure that you avoid the use of vague statements such as 'body language', 'facial expression' or 'eye contact'. These do not give a clear picture of the early warning signs so do not help, so be specific.

Finally, once we have all this information, then we can complete the final 3 sections. This part of the plan is the for the strategies. These are the interventions that we can use and there are 3 types of them – proactive (before any behaviours arise), de-escalation (to calm the situation) and reactive (emergency or crisis strategies). The bulk of the plan should be based around prevention which is why the proactive list should be the biggest. This should be an average of 70%. Remember the old saying again – what we focus on grows? If we focus on prevention and be proactive then this is the best way forward. A range of strategies will be looked at in Section 3.

h) 70% Prevention. These are strategies that are used proactively when the person is at a baseline state (remember the Crisis Cycle here – take a moment to go back to it if you need to).

Being proactive means that these strategies are put in place **before** any triggers, early warning signs or behaviours occur. In order for behaviour change to take place, these strategies should, ideally, comprise around 70% of your plan and daily work practice. In other words, 70% of our time should be focused on prevention of triggers and addressing the person's needs. If we do this then the person is less likely to use challenging behaviour to get their needs met.

i) 20% De-escalation. This section notes the de-escalation or calming strategies to put in place as early as possible after a trigger event or when the early warning signs are present.

Typically, these should be around 20% of the plan as these strategies will not change behaviours. They are calming techniques only so we should try not to spend all of our time de-escalating. Instead, focus on the 70% prevention and not getting to this point.

j) 10% Crisis strategies. This sets out what to do if all other strategies (i.e. the 70% prevention and 20% de-escalation) have failed and the challenging behaviour has occurred. In other words, these are the emergency strategies.

In summary, the 70/20/10 model is what we use to ensure that the balance is right. The main focus must be on prevention. If we don't focus on this then we will struggle to get a change.

Case study - Elise:

Elsie was observed to walk in the corridors, stop and then push her walking frame into the legs of others who were passing by or into the doorframes and walls. When we observed Elsie's behaviour, we noticed a subtle difference in the way she was using the frame.

When walking, the frame remained in contact with the floor. When standing, Elsie would slightly lift the frame and move it back and forth in front of her. Elsie would also move the frame back and forth rapidly. This behaviour appeared to indicate the rocking of a pushchair and possibly sweeping or vacuuming.

Having researched Elsie's life history, Elsie was introduced to doll therapy. She also used a lightweight carpet sweeper, when she was seated, to replicate 'hoovering'

Elsie would put the doll in the front basket of the walking frame and keep this with her. She also had a cot and drawer in her bedroom where the doll would 'sleep'.

See Page 145 for tips on introducing Doll Therapy

Here is a summary of a positive behaviour support plan as an example:

What's The Message

Example extract:
Positive Behaviour Support Plan
Name: Elsie XXXXXXXX
Page 1

Name: Elsie XXXXX	
Date: 12th January XX	Review date: 31st January XX
History: past hobbies, past employment, family, friends, interesting facts:	
Elsie was born in South Wales and lived there until she was 25. Elsie was married to Albert for 45 years. Albert died last year from bowel cancer. Elsie doesn't have any children. Elsie worked in a care home, as a housekeeper, for over 12 years.	
Likes:	**Dislikes:**
Elsie enjoys reminiscing about her past and talking about her husband. Elise likes chocolate, lemonade, stout, cake. Elise prefers to spend time in her room in the morning.	Elise does not like sausages, beans or tomato-based foods., Elsie does not like anyone touching her feet and her feet being cold.
Diagnosis/medical Information:	
Angina, previously suffered a stroke. Slight visual impairment Vascular Dementia: difficulties may include language, thinking, problem solving and reasoning. Frequent urinary tract infections (UTI's).	
Support strategies	
Behaviours identified:	
Elsie will push her walking frame into other people's legs or into the door frame or wall. Key times are morning and late afternoon	
What's the message? tangible, escape, social interaction, sensory?	
Elise is currently communicating a need of *Social Interaction* and *Tangible* through her behaviours. These behaviours are currently being displayed in the corridor, dining room and communal areas.	

Positive Behaviour Support plan - Example

Triggers	Early warning signs:
Not having meaningful activity and feeling bored Crowds and noisy environments	Elsie may clench her fists and talks faster or louder. Elsie's Welsh accent becomes more noticeable and her lip curls up at the edge

Actions used to prevent the behaviours
(70% baseline strategies):

Walking Frame: Observations carried out with Elsie have identified 2 reasons for moving her walking frame back and forth, namely:

a) When moved back and forth rapidly, we believe this motion replicates housework (hoovering or sweeping). Encourage Elsie to sit and use the lightweight carpet sweeper. Ask Elsie about the jobs that she used to do. Show Elsie pictures and use memory books to support discussion. Promote a sense of purpose for Elsie and offer her the opportunity to carry out domestic chores around the home – dusting objects, folding sheets etc.

b) When the walking frame is being lifted and then moved back and forth, this motion replicates pushing a pram. In this case, ensure Elsie's doll is available and in the basket of the frame.

Actions used to de-escalate the behaviours
(20% de-escalation strategies):

In response to early warning signs, consider redirection and calming techniques such as offering to help clean the house, wash the baby or look at photos of Albert.

Actions used to react to the behaviours
(10% crisis strategies):

Clear the area if behaviour becomes a danger to others
Avoid planting a suggestion of behaviour (i.e. don't throw the frame)

We will explore some different types of strategies in the next chapter because, at this stage, we cannot even start to consider any strategies until we first gather information on these 2 areas:

1.   The message behind or function of the behaviour

2.   What stage the person is at on the crisis cycle

Taking each of these points in turn:

To illustrate how to complete this part of the exercise, let's use an example. George is hitting out regularly at others. Which message would it be: Tangible? Escape? Social Interaction? Sensory?

There would be different strategies required depending on the message behind George's hitting. For example, if the message was:

a) Social Interaction - If George is trying to gain attention or interaction by hitting out at others then you may need to show George an alternative way for him to gain the attention, such as

- Behaviour modification to gently tap your arm instead
- Use a communication sign or verbally ask you
- Look at any key times when this is happening and go in to see George first (before any behaviours arises)

b) Escape or avoidance – if the behaviour is a need to avoid something or someone then you could perhaps:

- Show him a way to communicate how to stop something they don't like
- Stop doing the activity all together or try an alternative

c) Tangible – if George's hitting is to gain an item he wants or needs then:

- Make sure he has regular access to what he needs
- Help him to get something for himself where possible and make sure he knows where things are kept and that these are labelled clearly.

d) Sensory – if George is hitting himself for a sensory need, then maybe consider:

- A referral to a specialist such as an Occupational Therapist (OT) who can do a sensory assessment to clarify specific sensory needs
- Be creative! Use a substitute – a tambourine instead of hitting their leg or something that has a similar texture or feel.
- Make sure the substitute is assessed for any risk and then regularly available for him. (see Page 165 for more information on Substitute Skills)

In summary, for us to establish what the underlying message to the behaviour we must gather as much information as possible about what is happening, when, where and with whom when the challenging behaviour occurs.

There are a variety of ways that this information can be gathered in order for us to do this, including the most common:

- Interviews with other professionals, families or carers

- Direct observation of the person

- Behaviour Recording Charts, and

- 'Antecedent, Behaviour, Consequence' (ABC) Charts.

Next, let's look at two of these tools mentioned above – Behaviour Recording Charts and ABC Charts.

2. Behaviour Recording Charts

These charts can be used as a quick 'snap shot' of a **single** behaviour. This will enable you to see if there is a pattern of events or places when/where the behaviour is occurring. It is the first step of recording (before we start ABC charts).

Here is an example of a Behaviour Recording Chart that we use in our professional work:

Behaviour Recording Chart

Person's name:					Establishment:		
Behaviour identified:					When behaviour is exhibited, please specify exact time and frequency within the time slot		

Week Commending ...../...../......	10am	11am	Midday	1pm	2pm	3pm	4pm
Mealtimes							
Monday							
Tuesday							
Wednesday							
Thursday							
Friday							
Saturday							
Sunday							

The first section in the chart will list:

- The person's name,

- The behaviour being displayed. If there are multiple behaviours being displayed then do not use a Behaviour Recoding Chart, ABC Charts should be completed instead (see ABC Charts overleaf). The description of the behaviour should be clearly defined. For example, rather than saying 'aggression' which does not give us a clear description of the behaviour, it is better to be specific such as 'kicks out at others'.

The grid part of the chart is for recording (days and times can be changed to suit your own need):

- How many times the behaviour occurs in that time frame?

- Who was around at the time (initials only are needed)

- Where did the behaviour happen?, and

Recording mealtimes on this chart might establish whether the behaviour is around tangible needs, such as food or drink?

If this Behaviour Recording Chart doesn't highlight any patterns or anything obvious (or if there are multiple behaviours), then it may mean that we need a bit more in-depth information. This can be obtained by completing an Antecedent Behaviour Consequence (ABC) Chart.

3. Antecedent Behaviour Consequence (ABC) Charts

An **A**ntecedent **B**ehaviour **C**onsequence (ABC) Chart records more detail than the Behaviour Recording Chart such as the events that are occurring around the behaviours – what was said and done, when, how and by whom etc.

- "A" - **antecedent** - the event or activity that immediately precedes the challenging behaviour.

- "B" – **behaviour** – the observed challenging behaviour, and,

- "C" - **consequence** - the event/s that immediately follows the challenging behaviour

In our professional work, we use a chart that looks like this:

ABC RECORD OF BEHAVIOUR

Name:				BEHAVIOUR/S:	

Date/ Time:	Situation/ Conditions	Antecedent:	Behaviour:	Consequence:	Identified Need
	Place People Personal conditions Environmental conditions	What happened before the behaviour?	What did person do?	What did you do? What did the person do?	*Tangible* *Escape* *Sensory* *Social* *Interaction*

Remember that, with an ABC Chart, we are recording what we see and hear and not any interpretation of the behaviour – in essence we are recording the facts as we see them. Try to record information as soon as possible following a behaviour. This will ensure it is fresh in your mind and as accurate as possible.

Whilst there is a lot of information below on how to complete this chart, it doesn't have to be pages and pages long – keep it concise and simple!

Looking at the ABC Chart from left to right, this is the information that needs recording:

a)   **Date/Time:** This section is really important to help you establish whether there is a pattern to the behaviour, either time of day, day of the week or both.

b)   **Situation and Conditions:** This section needs to describe where the behaviours occurred. For example, was it a specific room in the home – kitchen, dining area or outside at the shopping centre near a certain shop. Behaviours are more likely to occur under certain *conditions* so we also need to be clear on the context of the situation. These conditions increase the likelihood of triggers and challenging behaviour because the person is unable to cope with that particular 'situation' or 'condition'.

There are two types of conditions: **Personal and Environmental.**

- **'Personal Conditions'** relate to how the person is feeling.
- **'Environmental Conditions'** describe the context in which the behaviour occurs

Personal	Environmental
Sweating	Hot/Cold
Upset	Crowded
Excited	Noisy
Can you list any others?	Can you list any others?
. . . .	. . . .
Turn to Page 200 for a suggested list	Turn to Page 200 for a suggested list

Triggers can happen when there is a clash of 'personal' and the 'environmental' conditions. For example, the person was tired, is known not to like loud noises (personal) and is sitting in a crowded, busy area (environmental). If there is a clash of the personal conditions and the environmental then this increases the likelihood of a trigger to behaviours. This is demonstrated in the following diagram:

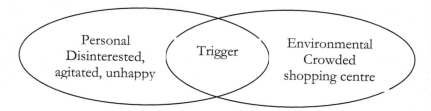

For example, if you take the personal condition of 'disinterested, agitated, withdrawn, unhappy', and this clashes with a busy environment or a noisy crowded shopping centre, then resulting behaviours we may see could be the person communicating the need to get away from the environment (escape and avoidance).

I'm sure it wouldn't surprise you to learn that challenging behaviour is more likely in challenging environments, such as the examples below:

Environmental	Which can impact on the personal setting:
High levels of social control or abuse	Low self-worth, fear, anger, frustration, loneliness, isolation
Low levels of social contact – loss of family friends or familiar faces	Isolation, uncertainty, anxiety
Lack of privacy	Resentment, embarrassment
No opportunity for personal items to be available	Not feeling welcome or at home, feeling unsafe
Lack of routine or unstructured	Confusion, frustration, anger

It is important, therefore, to think about the impact of the environment and what we can do to reduce a potential clash. For example, if there is noise outside and the person is distracted or cannot cope with this, then try playing calming music inside to block out the background chaos or, even better, see if the person would like to use headphones.

c) Antecedent

This is the events that happen **before** the behaviour occurs. If you've only been with the person a short while when the behaviour happens then it may mean that you need a little bit more information about what was happening before your involvement. You may need to dig a little deeper to find out what happened earlier by asking other people who were with the person. Questions to consider would be:

- What activity was the person and others doing?
- Were they receiving any attention from others? If so, who?
- What was the communication being used at the time?
- Were there any demands such as 'can you put your coat on'? Can you wash your hair? Let's go to the toilet?
- Did the person have any food or drink?
- Were there any signs of distress or discomfort?

d)   Behaviour

Once again, this should describe the behaviour in precise detail, for example, not to say 'aggression' but 'person hit my arm twice causing a red mark'. Within this section, you should also include information about the:

- *frequency* e.g. hits head with fist three times and kicks the floor
- *duration* - how long the behaviours lasted overall and also
- *intensity* – this could be a measure of how intense the behaviour is on a scale of 1-5 (e.g. hit head very hard which would be an intensity level of 5 or caused bruising to left side of head).

Remember to record all behaviours that you see, for example: X was screaming and shouting, X kicked my leg 3 times causing bruising and scratched another resident's arm which drew blood.

Different challenging behaviours could be for very different needs. For instance, the kicking could be for escape or avoidance from the person or from an activity that is due to come up, the scratching could be for sensory stimulation – watching the blood on the person's arm or feeling the skin under their nails.

e)   Consequence

This is the action that happens immediately after the behaviour occurs. Examples could be:

- What were the actions and responses of the person and others – both physical and verbal?
- Did the person receive attention from others? If so, who and how – undesired or positive?
- What was the person moved to another area or were activities provided?
- Was anything removed from the area?

And finally - Drum roll….. This is what it is all about….

f)   What's the message?

This is what we are ultimately looking to identify. If we don't get the this correct then we cannot implement a truly person centred plan for dealing with the behaviour.

Remember, just because the person has a diagnosis of Dementia does not mean that we are unable to support them to meet their needs without the use of challenging behaviour.

If a person can learn to use behaviour to get their needs met, they can learn how to get their needs met without the use of behaviour.

Section

Three

Strategies for

Positive Behaviour

Support

This section will cover the 3 categories of strategies that would be recorded in the PBS plan – in other words, cog 3: **what can be done?** These are:

70% Prevention strategies: This category will be used at a baseline state, i.e. before the trigger. They are strategies that ensure the person's needs and wants are met. These strategies are the most important in our PBS plans because they help to reduce, or eradicate, the behaviours of concern.

20% De-escalation strategies are used to calm the situation and are used after the trigger event and as soon as early warning signs are evident.

10% Crisis, or Emergency strategies. The strategies at this point are limited due to the risk situation. The overall purpose, therefore, of the PBS plan is not to get to this (or the 20%) stage as we hope to focus our work practice, and support, in that 70% area!

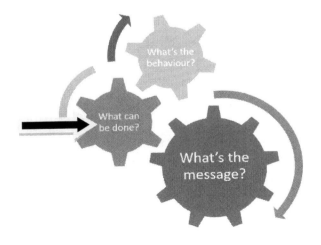

Chapter Five  70%

Let's start with you....

Self-Awareness and Self Control

Part 1: Self-Awareness

Everyone thinks of changing the world, but no one thinks of changing himself.

Leo Tolstoy: a Russian writer

The way you get to know yourself is by the expressions on other people's faces, because that's the only thing that you can see, unless you carry a mirror about.

*(Gil Scott-Heron: American musician and author, known primarily for his work as a **spoken word** performer in the 1970s and '80s)*

It may seem strange to think that the first of our strategies is going to be about turning the mirror on ourselves. It really is the starting point though. We have to firstly consider what role we play in all this? Are our actions, and the way we behave, contributing to triggers or challenging behaviours in others? The answer to this question is, no doubt, yes.

Therefore, we really need to consider how aware we are of ourselves. In terms of self-awareness, we like to think there are two types of people:

 Garlic People *and* Baked Bean People

Let us explain. Have you ever eaten a meal that is laden with garlic? What happens the following day? Generally speaking you have no idea of the garlic odour which is impacting on all those around you. Others can smell the garlic odour but you're oblivious to it.

However, if you have eaten a meal with lots of baked beans then you are totally aware of the impact you are having on others around you. I'll leave this to your imagination!

The reason we use this analogy is to help you think about whether you are really aware of your own behaviours and feelings and, ultimately, the impact you have on others – i.e. are you the baked bean person? Or do you go around leaving a trail of bad feeling behind you and have no idea of the impact you are having with your own behaviour – i.e. the garlic person. Which one do you think you are? Do you have enough self-awareness to even realise this?

Self-awareness is, in essence, knowing what 'makes you tick' and having a good understanding of your feelings and how you behave. It is also about understanding how your behaviour will impact on those around you.

It's not easy to turn the mirror on ourselves in order to reflect on our feelings and behaviours and to ask really tough questions about whether we reacted appropriately.

Maybe we took things personally and became over-sensitive or we came across as aggressive in our body language. Sometimes, it is easier for us to look at others and judge what others are doing, than to look at ourselves.

Self-awareness is important through all the stages of the Crisis Cycle but, most importantly, at the Trigger stage. If you can be aware of how you are behaving and feeling at this point, then the Limbic System hasn't fully taken over yet so you have more chance of remaining in control and avoiding the 'Amygdala hijack'. The further you go up towards crisis, the lower your self-awareness becomes.

What can be done?

a) **Recognise your emotions.** This is the first step to increasing your self-awareness - the ability to recognise a feeling as it happens. Try to develop the habit of monitoring your feelings from moment to moment. If you can recognise what 'pushes your buttons' and what you are feeling, then you should be able to know when to regulate and control what you are feeling.

b) **Understand how you come across to others.** Consider how you portray yourself to the other person through your communication. This is what and how you say it **(vocal)** and how you act **(visual).**

Vocal: The Vocal element of our communication is the words that we are saying and our voice tone.

Verbal

Voice tone relates to the 'musical' aspects of our voice, i.e. pitch, volume, pace, intonation and emphasis. I'm sure many of us have, at some point, been told *"It's not what you said but how you said it"*. Consider this example and how each one could have a different meaning:

"I didn't say you stole the money" Simple enough to understand, hey?

But now let's change the tone and intonation of some of the words to see how this might affect how it is heard by the recipient:

What you said   **Possible interpretation**

"***I*** didn't say you stole the money". . . . . Someone else said it

"I didn't ***say*** you stole the money" . . . . .I emailed everyone instead!

"I didn't say ***you*** stole the money" . . . . but I think your friend did!

"I didn't say you ***stole*** the money" . . . . but it was in your pocket!

"I didn't say you stole the ***money***". . . . but I do think you stole my watch!

Emotions are also conveyed by your voice tone - boredom, excitement, enthusiasm and interest are all examples. So, the message is clear: be aware of your voice tone as this is crucial when using calming techniques, for example, as it also shows others how you are feeling.

Visual :

"I speak 2 languages - English and Body" Mae West

The visual elements of how we communicate are wrapped up in our body language. But what do we mean by 'body language'?

The Oxford English Dictionary (revised 2005) definition is:
"Body language – noun - the conscious and unconscious movements and postures by which attitudes and feelings are communicated [for example]: his intent was clearly expressed in his body language"

Some more obvious examples of body language include:

- how we position our bodies – relaxed, rigid, arms folded

- our facial expressions – smiling, sad, clenched teeth

- our eyes movements, focus and expression – fixed eyes or looking away

- how we touch ourselves and others – picking at skin, playing with hair

- how our bodies connect with objects such as pens, clothing etc.

- our breathing – fast, slow... and

- where our body is in relation to others (often known as 'personal space')

As with recognising how you feel, it is also important to have some self-awareness of how you are communicating visually through your body language.

Body language is especially crucial when we meet someone for the first time as we generally form our opinions of someone very quickly upon meeting them.

There have been various research studies over the years on the time it takes to form a first impression. This has ranged from 30 seconds (According to Ros Taylor, author of the book "Confidence in Just Seven Days") to 15 seconds (research team: Toldeo University). Whichever research we consider, the fact remains that, before we even open our mouth to speak, our body language has given away the first impression of us!

When we recognise how we are portraying ourselves through our own body language then we become better able to refine and improve what our body 'says' about us.

Putting this all together, let's put the visual and vocal elements of communication together:

If someone ran into a room with a panicked expression on their face and shouted "FIRE!!", what would you do? Head for the nearest exit? Well, probably, yes.

However, what if that person just strolled in, sat down, yawned and with a slight grin shouted "Fire". Would you feel there was a sense of urgency about this? Would you be less likely to head for the exit? What do you think?

The fact is, for both of these examples, the spoken words (vocal communication) indicate the danger of a fire.

However, if there is a mis-match between what we are saying and what we portray through our body language, then people are more likely to believe the visual elements (i.e. what we see).

Have you ever tried to portray that you are feeling calm but there are the 'give-away' signs of gritted teeth, clenched fists and staring eyes? Here, there is a clear mis-match between what you're saying and how you appear to the other person.

What do you think they will believe? The fact is, it will be the visual elements of your body language. When there is a mis-match, it is this part that will give the game away and show the true picture!

Consider these photos. Do you believe what they say?

Having good self-awareness (or being a baked bean person) would mean that there is less likely to be a mis-match to what you are saying and how you are actually portraying yourself with your body language.

c) **Gain feedback from others** Another thing you can do to increase self-awareness is to be open to feedback from others (preferably people you trust) to help you better understand how you come across. As we have said earlier, it is not easy to turn the mirror on ourselves. Sometimes we need the help of others in order for us to learn about how we are being perceived. We can use a model called the Johari Window to help us get a better understanding of this.

The Johari Window Model was created by Joseph Luft and Harry Ingram in 1955 to help understand our self-awareness. There's a saying that paraphrases the Johari Window Model:

"If one person calls you a horse, ignore them. If 3 people call you a horse, look in the mirror. If 5 people call you a horse, buy a saddle."

This basically means that if there are enough people telling you something, you may want to listen to them! Within the Johari Window Model there are 4 window panes:

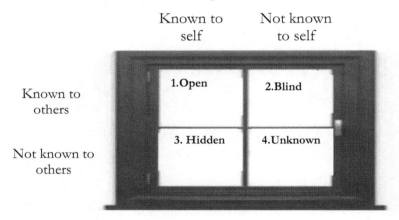

Pane 1: Open: Traits that are known to self and others – these are out in the open and are the things you and other people know about you. You may have shared with everyone that you have a fear of spiders or that you are shy when you first meet people.

Pane 2: Blind: Unknown to self, known to others. These are the things about you that you are not aware of, but other people see. This pane is probably the most sensitive to provide feedback on, especially if it's not a positive characteristic!

You may be blissfully unaware that your lip curls up every time you get angry or that you fidget a lot when eating your food – you might not be aware but others are.

Pane 3: Hidden: Known to self, not known to others. These are things that you know about yourself but others do not. The hidden self could be feelings, talents, information (secrets), fears or anything that a person does not make known to others.

Pane 4: Unknown: Not known to self, not known to others. These are the things about you that both you and others do not know. This area represents the opportunity to explore new ideas about yourself. You never know - you might be good at horse riding or bell ringing. If you don't try it then you'll never know.

So, the Johari Window is a useful tool in self-analysis: after all, you cannot consciously change what you don't know. The key is to be open to the feedback other people are giving you. Everybody knows at least somebody that has some glaring 'blind spots' and just won't listen. This model can be applied to just about any area where there is more than 1 person (business, family, etc.). You could use this to analyse emotions, personality traits, etc.

Johari Window Exercise

Here's an exercise that the founders of the Johari Window Model came up with which could be a good starting point.

List 1: Pick the 5-6 characteristics that represents yourself.

List 2: Then have 5-6 other people pick 5-6 characteristics that represent you from list 2.

From there you can build your own **simple Johari Window Model.** In other words, when all your lists are complete, compare what you have put and what others list. Are there any characteristics that match? Do others see you the same (or similar) characteristics as you see? Are there any common themes?

List 1

able	dependable	intelligent	patient	sensible
accepting	dignified	introverted	powerful	sentimental
adaptable	energetic	kind	proud	shy
bold	extroverted	interesting	quiet	silly
brave	friendly	logical	reflective	smart
calm	giving	loving	relaxed	spontaneous
caring	happy	mature	religious	sympathetic
cheerful	helpful	modest	responsive	tense
clever	idealistic	nervous	searching	trustworthy
complex	independent	observant	assertive	warm
confident	ingenious	organised	witty	open

Categorise '*Open*' as the traits that at least one other person identified that you also identified

Categorise '*Blind*' as traits that others have listed and you did not

Categorise '*Hidden*' as traits you listed that others did not

Categorise the rest of the traits as *'Unknown'*

To be effective, be sure to analyse the positive and negative qualities! Use feedback to your advantage, it can pay dividends. The Johari Window can also be used as a tool to examine unknown areas that need to be developed. It's generally better and easier to have your friends or people you trust give you feedback on these kinds of issues.

So, here's a quick list of "negative qualities" to get you started.

List 2

blasé	distant	inane	needy	timid
boastful	dispassionate	inattentive	pushy	unethical
brash	dull	incompetent	dramatic	unhappy
callous	embarrassed	inflexible	panicky	unhelpful
chaotic	foolish	insecure	passive	unimaginative
childish	glum	insensitive	predictable	unreliable
cold	hostile	intolerant	rash	vacant
cowardly	humourless	irrational	selfish	vicious
creepy	ignorant	irresponsible	self-satisfied	vulgar
cruel	impatient	lethargic	smug	weak
cynical	imperceptive	loud	Arrogant	withdrawn

Part 2: Emotional Self-Control

Anger is an acid that can do more harm to the vessel in which it is stored than to anything on which it is poured. (Mark Twain)

Emotional self-control is about having the ability to calm yourself down and regulate your emotions when you can feel yourself getting angry or upset (or any intense flood of emotions).

In order to do this, however, you first need to recognise the signs that you are starting to have a flood of negative emotions. You may notice signs such as your heart beating faster, you breath more quickly or your stomach starts to churn. This is your own body reacting to the emotions and telling you to prepare for action (remember the Crisis Cycle). The minute you start to notice these internal signals, then you need to act before the Limbic system starts to take over and you become flooded with emotions with no thinking or reasoning involved. The best thing you can do at this point is to walk away the situation. However, this is not always possible, so here are some tips to think about:

What can be done?

a) Control your Breathing. Part of changing our emotional state involves dealing directly with the physical changes. Physical changes are often led by the way we breathe. For instance, anger and anxiety can 'surface' if we are breathing quicker with shallow breaths.

Therefore, it is sometimes possible to control this situation by taking control of our breathing. Try one of the two techniques below next time you begin to feel angry or anxious:

i) Hold your breath for five seconds. This will 'reset' your breath. Now breathe in slowly until you feel that your lungs are full of air. Then breathe out *even more slowly*. Whilst doing this, imagine that you are breathing out pure rest and relaxation. Keep doing this and remember it's the *out-breath* that will calm everything down. 3 to 4 deep breaths will oxygenate the brain. (Think of your whole Limbic system being 'cooled' with oxygen.) This will help to switch the thinking and reasoning part of the brain, putting the Neocortex back into action.

ii) A second breathing exercise is to breathe in 'colour'. As a self-calmer this can be useful but a word of warning – you need to close your eyes for this one. This will not be very useful if you are supporting someone at the time! To start this exercise, close your eyes and take a slow, deep breath. Whilst you inhale, imagine you are breathing in a particular colour – deep rich purple for example.

With every breath in, now imagine this colour flowing through your entire body (not just your lungs). Start at the tips of your toes and continue right up to the top of your spine.

b) Refocus your thoughts. Other approaches you can try are to redirect your thoughts and focus on something different. Have you have ever immersed yourself in something that takes a great deal of focus – Sudoku, crosswords, computer games, favourite film etc? Did it help to switch off the Limbic and those emotional thoughts? It should do as the Limbic is now operating at a secondary level and the higher functioning part of the brain is in action!

c) 'Anchor' your emotions. Anchoring is a term used in Neuro Linguistic Programming (NLP) which was founded in the early 1970s by a linguistic Professor from the University of California, John Grinder.

The term 'Anchor' is our emotional response to some form of stimuli. This could be the sight of a holiday photograph which may put you in a good mood (if it was a positive experience, of course). The sound of a friend's voice on your voicemail may give a feeling of happiness. The feeling of safety when given a hug by your mum or dad. The feeling of dread if your boss asks you to attend an out of the blue 'catch up' meeting. These feelings just happen naturally to us in response to our memories and what is happening around us. They are therefore known as 'natural anchors' because, quite simply, they happen naturally.

As well as naturally occurring anchors, we can also learn to 'set' our own anchors to change our emotional state. This technique is based on the earlier memories we had of being in that particular state.

The first step is to identify the emotional state you want to trigger through the anchor you create. For example: calmness, relaxed, enthusiastic, energetic, happy. This step is crucial.

Next, recall a powerful memory that triggers this emotional state. Don't forget to include as many of your senses as possible within this memory - the sights, sounds, tastes, touch alongside the feelings. For example, if you are looking to anchor the feeling of relaxation, then it could be that you had a recent massage or facial during a visit to a spa. Think deeply about the event and your emotions at the time:

- what did you *see* (the candles, the colour of the room)

- what did you *hear* (the soft music, the sound of the birds or sound of the ocean)

- what did you *feel* (the touch of the oils, the massage)

- what did you *smell* (the aromas of the oils, the scent of the candles)?

Think about these things as if it was happening 'in the here and now'.

When the memory and emotions are at their peak, anchor this with a unique hand movement – something sufficiently different from the way you normally hold or use your hands (you should also make your hand movement something that can be done discretely). The feelings are now anchored to the physical movement of the hand gesture.

Try this for yourself and list the positive memories and anchors:

Emotional state I want to trigger	The memory that I will use to trigger this state	The Anchor I will use to 'fire up' the emotion
Energetic	Climbing Mount Snowdon. The air is clear, the sky is blue, the views are breath-taking. I feel on top of the world	Right thumb pressed against my right index finger

Some people find anchoring very powerful the first time they experience it, while others need more practice. It is a personal thing.

d) Reject the negative self-talk. Most people don't even realise they are doing this but we are always interpreting the situations we find ourselves in. It's our 'inner voice' that determines how we perceive a situation. Psychologists call this our 'self-talk'. More often than not, this is reasonable – 'I need to cook dinner later', 'I'm looking forward to home-time'.

However, sometimes it is negative about yourself and others. 'I'm going to fail', 'I can't do this', 'it's personal against me', or 'he's doing this to wind me up'. Try changing this self-talk to more positive thoughts such as 'it's tough at the moment, but it will pass', 'she does this with everyone and it's not about me', 'he's just doing this because he is upset right now.

To summarise,

"All that we are is the result of what we have thought.
The mind is everything. What we think we become."
(Buddha)

Our emotional state can create a cycle of behaviours which can be described as *behaviour breeds behaviour*. This statement comes from research known as 'Betari's Box', the origin of which is unknown.

The model shows a cycle of emotions and impact on behaviour. Let's start with looking at the top of the diagram 'my emotion' and follow the link to 'my behaviour'. If we are feeling motivated, happy and positive (my emotion) then we are more likely to smile and laugh (my behaviour). However, if we're feeling negative, upset or angry, then the reverse is true, in that we may become impatient, shout, become argumentative or even cry.

Looking at this cycle, 'my' behaviour (be it positive or negative) can then affect the people around us. Firstly, my behaviour may now generate 'your' emotion which, in turn, affects how you may respond and behave towards me.

If your response is negative in the way you feel then you may turn your negative behaviours back on me, and the conflict then starts to spiral. Although the concept of the Betari Box is quite simple, understanding it can help people learn to recognise when they're stuck in a negative cycle.

So, for behaviour breeds behaviour, **what can be done?**

- Remember that your emotions, good or bad, are likely to affect those around you.

- If someone around you is behaving negatively, then remember that you have a choice in how you respond emotionally to that. Just because that person is negative to you doesn't mean that you have to be negative in your response.

- The next time you're in a bad mood, try to stop what you're doing. Take a few minutes to reflect and become self-aware about why you're feeling negative and how this is coming across to others (through your own body language and behaviour). Consciously decide to 'press the reset button' of the cycle by focusing on something positive.

Remember, it is very likely that the person with Dementia is still able to recognise and interpret body language, facial expressions, the tone and inflection of your voice even if their understanding of the spoken word has been lost.

We can often make assumptions – quite wrongly - that, deep down, the person with Dementia knows they are in a care setting and so ought to accept all that happens to and around them. Often, because of this assumption, we don't offer adequate explanation, or the communication we use may be too complex, because we assume that the person has understood.

We can also make other assumptions such as a person is more (or less) dependent and in a constant state of confusion and is not able to enjoy life.

We should never assume. It is often our behaviour that can make the difference to people's lives. Remember: *Behaviour breeds behaviour!*

Chapter Six

Communication and Dementia

Part 1

Have you ever experienced a communication barrier? Maybe when you have been overseas on holiday and you want to order food or a drink (in other words, those basic tangible needs) and you are faced with a communication barrier? So, you look at the menu, which is set out in a different language (French, for example), and you simply don't understand anything you read. But, hey, then you see 'Steak Tartare'. OK....that sounds nice – right? The meal is delivered to you, only to be presented with uncooked red meat. Oh, it doesn't end there. Also... an uncooked egg (yes, that is a Steak Tartare and this is a true story)! How do you feel? Frustrated? Disappointed? Angry? Humiliated? Helpless? .... Hungry!? Maybe all of the above feelings because it was an expensive mistake and, you might think, raw and inedible!

We all have needs. We have established this referencing Maslow's Hierarchy of Needs in Section One. But what if you are unable to communicate your needs, wants or wishes? Or you believe that you <u>are</u> communicating them but others don't seem to understand you. Or you are simply unable to recognise what you want anymore. Just because a person is finding it communicating difficult, it doesn't mean they should live feeling socially excluded or isolated. Remember how it would have felt in the restaurant?!

Underpinning all of our strategies is the need for the correct form of communication. The strategies used on the PBS plan will need to be adapted to suit the person's communication strengths and difficulties. Good communication will also depend on other factors such as:

- How well the person can hear
- How well the person can see
- How comfortable they're feeling
- How well they can express themselves to others
- How quickly they can process the information they are given
- How interested and motivated they are to communicate

With this in mind, take a look at the list of communication methods below. The list is jumbled up in the wrong order. In the box to the right, write down what, **in general**, you think is the easiest form of communication for a person with Dementia through to what you feel would be the most difficult? If you don't understand some of the terms used in the communication list below, these will be explained throughout this chapter so you can come back to this exercise later.

- **Sign**
- **Written word**
- **Objects of reference**
- **Symbols**
- **Photographs**
- **Spoken word**
- **Line drawing**

This list is not exhaustive and will, of course, vary from person to person due to their diagnosis. Each person will have their own way of getting their message across and also of receiving information. As such, it is vital that each person is recognised as having their own particular way of communicating.

From this list, however, for Dementia, we would suggest that**, in general**:

a) **Objects of reference** can be the simplest method of communicating. These are, as the name implies, objects that have a particular meaning associated with them. For example, a toilet roll may be the object of reference for the toilet; a spoon may be a reference to breakfast; a cup for a drink. These objects give the person information about what is going to happen. The use of objects of reference, however, should be consistently used.

The objects should have relevance for that person. For example, showing a person a credit card (to represent the bank) may not be suitable if the person only recalls using a bank book. Objects should, therefore, be chosen sensitively, particularly with reference to personal care - a nappy, for example, would not be the best choice to indicate changing time, so perhaps a washing bag should be used instead.

Once a person understands what the object represents, they may then be able to indicate a choice by pointing with their finger or eyes.

b) Photographs can be used as the next best thing. It may be helpful to have them checked by a communication specialist (such as a Speech and Language Therapist) and create a 'bank' of them so that they are readily available.

c) Line drawing and symbols. The use of symbols and 'stick men' drawings can be very helpful in communicating information and supporting people's understanding.

d) Sign. There are several different sign language systems, including British Sign Language (BSL), MakatonTM, Signalong, Paget Gorman Signed SpeechTM and Signed Exact English.

e) Spoken word. Some people may be able to understand what is being said but it may need to be at a slow rate. If your speech is too complex or long sentences then this may make the person anxious. In response to this, the person may then start to repeat things that are being said so that they can store them in their memory whilst also processing what has been said.

If there is a lack of understanding of what is being said then this can lead to confusion and possibly frustration for the person, this, in turn, has the potential to result in behaviours. Remember, therefore, that this list is a generalised view of communication methods.

Part 2: Communication and Dementia: The 3 A's

For us to adjust our communication to be person-specific, we firstly need to understand more about the type of Dementia the person is diagnosed with, the stage and the level of understanding the person has.

In this part, let's consider **the '3 A's'** (Agnosia, Apraxia and Aphasia) and relate this to what we need to consider for our communication:

a) Agnosia

In this section, we will concentrate on 'visual and facial Agnosia'. The term Agnosia is actually translated from Greek as meaning 'absence of knowledge'.

Visual Agnosia occurs when the pathways connected from the Occipital Lobe to the Parietal/Temporal Lobes are damaged. The Occipital Lobe is receiving the visual information from the eyes OK, but cannot transfer the data received to the rest of the brain in order to understand the meaning of it.

This can, in the early stages, confuse the recognition of objects. For example, a person may use a toothbrush instead of a hairbrush or a spoon instead of a fork.

As the disease progresses, this could lead to a complete inability to recognise the purpose of objects and even to orientate themselves around their surroundings.

This could then mean that the person may sit at the table and then proceed to eat their food with their fingers even though there is a knife and fork next to their plate. Environmentally, the person may have difficulty locating their bedroom as they are unable to recognise their door or where it is in the building.

What can be done?

- **Use different senses:** Objects of reference can still be used here but change this and offer something for the person to touch, taste, smell or listen to. With the previous example of the fork, we could, perhaps, offer this to the person to feel as soon as they sit down to eat. If a person is not able to recognise their door keys then try placing them in the person's hands so that they can attempt to recognise them by touch or even the sound of the keys rattling.

- Don't forget the **sense of smell**. If there is a distinctive odour to the object then try tapping into the sense of smell to support recognition; the smell of mint for toothpaste, for example.

- **Mirroring behaviour.** In other words, using your body language to demonstrate what the object is used for. At mealtimes, try sitting with the person at the table, using the fork to eat or stand next to them and brush your teeth to demonstrate the use of the toothbrush.

When brushing their teeth, stand next to the person and pretend to brush your teeth, placing a toothbrush in their hand too. Once again, use short sentences to describe what you are doing and prompt the person to do the same. This will help them understand what the object is used for and then mirror, or copy, your behaviour.

- **Use of colour.** Colour can also be used (unless the person has been diagnosed as having colour Agnosia. This means that there is an inability to recognise the name and distinguish the type of colour). As an example, if the person is able to recognise colour and is confused about where their bedroom door is, could the door be decorated with an emblem to resemble their favourite football team? Could the door be labelled in a way that the person will recognise? Or be painted with the same features and colour as their old front door at home?

- **Limit options** and avoid having similar looking items close together. Instead of confusing matters with 3 types of cutlery on the table, try just having a spoon. Similarly, with clothes, just have one item at a time. With personal care, limit the amount of accessories that are in the bathroom and avoid having items that look the same placed together – for example, hairspray and deodorant. The person may end up with very sticky armpits!

- **Consider the person's environment.** For example, the 'clinical' look and feel of a bathroom in a residential setting for personal care tasks.

How different will this be from what the person was used to? Handrails, chrome and metal objects (such as moving and handling aids), flooring and décor can all be confusing and have the potential to trigger anxiety. In cases such as this, try using distraction techniques to divert the person's attention. Objects of reassurance can also be used very effectively as these are basically 'comforters' or sensory aids that the person holds on to in order to focus their attention and provide reassurance.

- Be mindful about the **dangers** of leaving **hazardous or toxic substances** around. This can also include medication. The person might mistake tablets for sweets or a bottle of bleach as a drink.

Whilst visual Agnosia is the inability to recognise objects, it is highly likely that this will also include people! In other words, **Prosopaganosia (face blindness)**:

Task:

Overleaf we have created a task which will attempt to cause chaos to your Occipital and Temporal Lobes and, therefore, create face blindness.

However, before you jump straight into the next page, please follow these simple instructions:

1.   Keep the book upright
2.   Keep your head straight – do not tilt your head to the side.

Now that you are ready. The task is to see if you can recognise the 'celebrities'. All we have done is removed their hair and turned them upside down!

Make your notes here:

a:

b:

c:

d:

e:

f:

Here you go, give it a try:

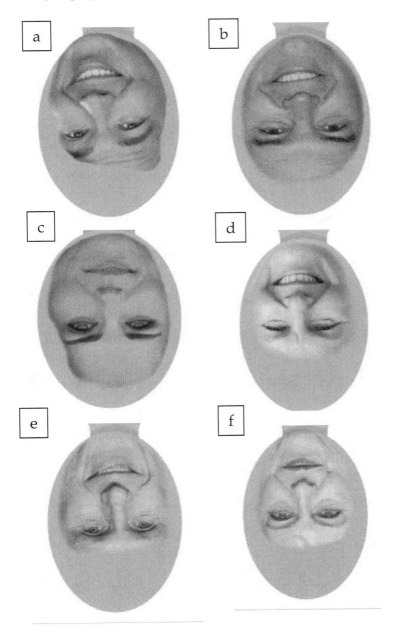

How did you do? Check out the answers on page 198

The exercise you have just undertaken gives you an idea of how face blindness might feel when the messages being passed through your eyes into your own Occipital Lobe get confused.

Face blindness, therefore, is the inability to recognise themselves or others and is therefore not as a result of memory loss. It is, instead, the breakdown of information supplied, by the eyes, to the Occipital Lobe which would, ordinarily, be able to translate and recognise who they have seen.

Gareth is supported to have a shave regularly throughout the week. He prefers to have a shave after he has had a shower. Gareth is settled throughout showering. Once he is dressed and sat in front of the bathroom mirror, he then has a towel placed on his shoulders. Gareth will lunge and shout at the mirror. Gareth does not recognise his reflection in the mirror so believes it to be that of another person. The mirror has now been removed from the bathroom.

Deidre is very sociable and chatty with others. When Deidre walks to the end of the corridor, she stops at the glass door and will start shouting and banging the door. Deidre thinks that her reflection is the image of her mother. Deidre does not have very good memories of her mother and is often heard shouting and accusing her mother of hurting her. The glass has now been frosted so that there isn't a reflection

Clive goes into other resident's bedrooms every day. He has a picture on his own bedroom door which was taken recently. Clive does not recognise himself in this picture so he is confused as to where his bedroom is. Clive has been a Manchester United support for all of his life. Clive now has a red door and a Manchester United emblem on it. Clive also has Man U bedding and curtains in his room. Clive now recognises his room!

In summary, challenging behaviour, in all of these examples, has been displayed by the person in order for them to communicate their message of escape or avoidance. This can be from another person or could even be themselves!

What can be done?

When you are supporting someone who has face blindness, or you suspect might have, these are some techniques and approaches you could try to help the person recognise you and others:

a) **Introduce yourself** each time you are in contact with the person. Avoid saying things like 'do you know who I am?' as this can cause anxiety and frustration if the person is unable to recognise you. Instead, say the person's name and then say 'it is ….. here'

b) **Use the senses**: once again, tapping into the person's other senses could help them to recognise others by touch, clothing that you regularly wear, hairstyle, sound of your voice or how you smell.

c) **Be consistent**. Try using the same perfume or deodorant, for example. If you wear glasses, then try to keep them on or off each time you meet the person (be consistent with whatever you choose). Try to keep your hairstyle the same rather than having hair in a ponytail one day and then loose the next. If you wear a hat, wear it consistently to minimise the change of confusion for the person.

b) Aphasia

Aphasia derives from the Greek word meaning 'speechlessness' and, therefore, means the inability to use or even understand language. The damage here comes from the Temporal and Frontal Lobes which helps to control speech and language. As with all forms of communication, we need to be able to express the language we use and then be able to understand, or receive, the language back. This is why there are two types of Aphasia. Quite simply:

Expressive: to be able to say (or express) and write the correct words in the correct formation, and
Receptive: to be able to understand (or receive) the information.

Signs that may be evident with aphasia could include:

- The person may say the wrong words - they may use a word that has a similar meaning or sounds similar such as tick-tock instead of clock or fair instead of hair

- The words may get jumbled up or may be completely irrelevant in context.

- They may make mistakes in grammar or leave out the small link words. For example, 'am going shops', instead of 'I am going to the shops'.

- The person's responses may also become 'long-winded' because they are unable to find the correct wording.

- Their speech may be slower than usual or hesitant and taking a lot of effort and may even include stuttering

- They may find it difficult to understand long sentences

- The person may also show signs of echolalia which means they repeat what another person has said. 'Echo' in Greek simply means to 'repeat' whilst 'lalia' means 'speech'. For example: a person is slapping their face and shouting. They are asked 'are you OK?' The echolalic response would be to continue to slap their face and repeat 'are you OK'.

- You may also see an increase in singing, swearing or cursing. This is because the left Hemisphere of the brain that controls the formal language has been damaged leaving the right Hemisphere more intact. The right Hemisphere controls speech that is more 'automatic' such as yes and no responses, singing and…. yes, swearing!

- As with Agnosia, this is not just related to objects. Aphasia can also impact on names which means that the person may get names of family or carers wrong.

What can be done?

- Remember the chapter on **self-awareness.** How are you coming across to the person? If the person cannot understand your verbal language, they can still recognise your body language (facial expression and gestures) and your voice tone and speed of speech. You need to consider, therefore, will the person feel reassured in your company?

- You can **demonstrate** the use of an object first, instead of using verbal instructions

- Use objects of reference or other **non-verbal signs** that the person may understand. For example, when giving a choice of bath or shower, use a flannel or shower head and see if they point or use photographs and point to one or the other to see if the person mirrors this.

- Try to eliminate any **background noise** so that the person is able to focus

- Try to get **confirmation** from the person that you are communicating correctly by either signing or saying 'Yes' or 'No'. This may be using a 'thumbs up' or 'thumbs down'.

- **Avoid correcting** the person as this can cause frustration

- **TV:** For a person with a language impairment, certain TV programmes may cause anxiety. This is because, although the person may not understand the words, they are still able to recognise the inflection and tone of other people's voices. They are also able to understand body language.

  If people are shouting and using aggressive posturing on TV (a certain daytime programme chat show - which seems to be regularly shown in residential settings - springs to mind here) then this will clearly cause confusion for the person and can be upsetting. In which case, try to observe for early warning signs of distress or confusion from the person.

- As the condition progresses, a person may become incoherent. Still ensure that communication is kept open and at an **adult level** – avoiding a patronising or child-like tone of voice. Remember the person has a communication difficulty and not impaired intelligence!

c) Apraxia

There are different types of apraxia but, for ease of understanding, this section is focusing on the general terms of Apraxia as the difficulty or inability to plan and coordinate movement in response to verbal instruction, even though the person may retain the physical ability do the task.

You may see that the person has completed the task previously, however, this may be due to what is known as 'spontaneous action'. This means that the task has been possible through habit (which doesn't take any processing thought). An example of this could be when a phone rings and you automatically pick up the receiver.

Complications, therefore, arise when the brain has to 'plan' the task and organise the sequence or instructions it received. Problems can occur with the 'working memory processing' in the brain or, in other words, processing the sequence of actions to a task. Therefore, certain activities for daily living (otherwise known as ADL's), that would have previously been a straightforward action (such as cooking, cleaning, ironing, washing or brushing your hair) now become complex actions.

This means that even a simple task (such as getting up from a chair) might be extremely complex to follow because it has a number of stages to it, for example:

- Feet positioned on the floor ready to stand
- Hands on the sides of the chair
- Shuffle forward
- Head forward, looking upwards
- Push up with the arms
- Lean forward
- Push up with legs
- Stand

According to different studies, it has been reported that there can be up to 13 different stages just for washing your hands and a massive 34 stages for getting dressed (Tappen 1994, Beck 1998).

Knowing this will help us understand that the many ADLs we carry out, with ease, are actually complex actions but our brain helps us to plan and process all this information so we can function. People with Apraxia will struggle with this.

Clearly, if we can help to improve people's ability to continue or contribute in part to their own ADL's, then this will help promote independence and, ultimately, a sense of wellbeing and worth (remember the fourth stage of Maslow).

What can be done?

- **Demonstrate**: the person may be able to imitate your movements, if shown. If this is proving difficult, then try using your own hands over their hands to guide the movement.

- **Promote concentration:** Create a quiet environment and try to avoid times when the person is tired or in discomfort.

- **'Chunk' the information:** This may mean that we offer one instruction at a time. Remember, a neurotypical working memory in the brain can process, on average, between 5 and 9 pieces of sequential information at a time. A person with a working memory deficit may not be able to process this length of information and may only be able to process 1 or, possibly, 2 'chunks' at a time.

- Use **visual communication aids** to show what is happening **now** and then what is happening **next**. Allow extra **time** for the person to process what they see.

It could be that the person enjoys baking, in which case you can take them through the sequence (this may mean using a visual picture chart or the objects to do so): get eggs, get milk, get bowl etc. Then, review the schedule throughout the baking process. For getting dressed, set out the items in front of the person in the set order of, socks, underwear, shirt, trousers - if this is their preferred sequence

- **Routine:** This is something that is needed by all of us to some degree. Think about how you get dressed in the morning. Do you have a set pattern? Socks first or underwear first, socks second? Do you like to have breakfast at a certain time or after certain tasks (such as washing or dressing)? Do you like your hair appointments on certain days, going for a walk at certain times or washing and drying dishes straight after mealtimes?

Remember, routines have probably been with the person since they were young and are no doubt established in their long-term memory. In which case, it could be reassuring to the person to keep their own personal routine as much as possible.

Changes to routine can be triggered by events such as holidays, birthdays or Christmas. Changes can also be daily 'transitions' such as moving between activities or from one situation to another. Examples include leaving the house to getting into the car, arriving at the shops, going into the shops, staff changeover etc. If the routine is known, record this information on the PBS plan so that everyone who supports the person can try to stick to it

- **Environmental conditions.** Think about the last time you moved things around in your home. I recall a time when I moved the kitchen clock to a different position in the room. The family moaned about it for weeks!

What about when you go on holiday and stay in a different bedroom? Is there a certain side of the bed that you like to get out of? Do you get confused when you need to visit the bathroom in the middle of the night and, half asleep, you end up in the wardrobe!

Muscle memory is when your brain has taught your muscles to respond in a certain way. For example, when you enter a dark room, and you are familiar with the location of the light switch, your muscle memory will remember the location so you can switch on the light without the need for sight.

In early stages of Dementia, muscle memory may still be intact so it is important for us to consider this and look at the set-up of the environment. Think about the position of the person's bed – do you know what side of the bed they like to get out of?

- Find **alternative ways** with less complex sequences. For example, rather than tying shoe laces, try Velcro straps instead.

- Try to keep the **person motivated** by offering words of praise and encouragement for completing stages of the task. Difficulties with carrying out the actions needed for daily living will, at times, lead to frustration for the person. This could mean the person wants to 'give up' on the task which might lead to a reliance on others to perform these tasks on their behalf, and the so the spiral continues.

- **Deterioration.** Be mindful that, as the disease progresses, longer-term memories of motor skills such as chewing, swallowing and walking will be affected.

Finally, if you are unsure about any aspects of apraxia, then keep a daily record of the difficulties the person is experiencing. You are then in a stronger position to discuss this with the person's GP to establish the type or any other underlying physical/medical factors.

Chapter Seven

Different types of Therapies

The term *complementary and alternative* therapies cover a large range of therapy types. Most people will generally recognise therapies such as aromatherapy, massage, herbal supplements or acupuncture, for example. Whilst these therapies are not a cure for the Dementia, they can be used to reduce symptoms and improve the person's quality of life. It may be helpful to consult with the person's Occupational therapist or GP about what, or if any, alternative therapies can complement the person's existing medical treatment plan.

1) Music therapy

Music is so personal that it can have a powerful impact on our emotions – both negative and positive. This is because music stimulates the creative side of the brain and the emotions that are attached to the memory of the music.

Think about a piece of music that you enjoy. If you haven't heard it for a while, and it gets played on the radio what does it take you back to? Well, Wham (Club Tropicana) takes me back to my younger years and holidays abroad, and I feel happy listening to it.

However, the opposite can also be true. Try playing a piece of music that has negative memories associated to it. This is why, in residential services, we ask that music is person-specific and not 'pumped' out of speakers in communal areas or the radio playing in the background with music that has no meaning.

With advances in technology, personal 'play lists' can be created for a person and they can have access to a whole library of their choice of music in something that is the size of a matchbox. This is truly person-centred and costs very little!

Want more evidence. Look on You Tube for a clip called 'Alive Inside' and the story of Henry. This demonstrates that music can not only stimulate the right Hemisphere of the brain (which is the creative side) but that stimulation jumps over 'the bridge' and triggers parts of the left Hemisphere too where the language is stored. So, where a person may struggle with language, they can become quite 'talkative'. Sit back and enjoy that clip – it's one of our favourites!

And music therapy goes much further than this. Music can encourage movement – foot tapping, hand swinging or dancing (seated or standing). This, in turn, stimulates alertness, can relive stress and has many other physical benefits that can come with movement and exercise.

Music can be used in a range of structured or even unstructured ways, either in a group session or individually, for example:

- Musicals or theatre or live performances (some theatres now advertise Dementia-friendly performances)
- Playing instruments or singing
- Listening to pre-recorded films or music

Finally, music can also be used to lower stimulation at times of the day when you want to promote relaxation (sundowning, for example).

And, let's not forget, that, once again, music therapy has the potential to benefit all of us and is not just reserved for those diagnosed with a Dementia!

2) Doll therapy

At this point, it might be helpful to recap to our earlier theory on Maslow's Hierarchy of Needs. More specifically, the need for social interaction, feelings of love and belonging (level 3) and the need for a sense of purpose (level 4).

Doll therapy can bring great benefit to some people with a diagnosis of Dementia and is sometimes used for people who are in the later stages of Dementia, or diagnosed with a mixed Dementia, as they are more likely to accept and care for the doll as a 'baby'.

We also need to factor in the background and history of the person if using doll therapy so that we can assess the opportunities it offers or, alternatively, any disbenefits. For example, is the person known to have liked being around children or babies? Maybe, however, they have had a traumatic experience that could be triggered by the introduction of a doll?

Are they exhibiting behaviours that are demonstrating that doll therapy would be of use? For example, Elsie, from our earlier case study, who was pushing her walking frame to simulate pushing a pram. In other words, we don't just introduce a doll to everyone. It is a therapy tool and, as such, needs careful assessment. Let's not forget too that this therapy is recognised for both males and females!

Wendy will remove her own faeces from the toilet and wrap it in toilet paper. Wendy will then 'cradle' the faeces and hide it under her bed so that staff do not remove it. When Wendy leaves the room, she will put her faeces on the windowsill so that her 'baby' can look out of the window:

Remember, Wendy's behaviours are valid for her. What's the message? Our behaviour assessment concluded 'social interaction'. Wendy believed the faeces to be her babies. This is another opportunity to introduce a substitute by using doll therapy. Wendy now cradles the doll and no longer scoops out her faeces from the toilet.

Doll therapy has been seen by some as undignified or infantilising the person and sometimes family members become upset to see their parent or relative interacting so closely with a 'toy'.

The Royal College of Nursing (2008) states that *'when dignity is present, people feel in control, valued, confident, comfortable and able to make decisions for themselves'.*

Therefore, if a person with Dementia benefits from looking after a doll then this is their choice which, in our view, promotes value, confidence and comfort.

We also have to recognise and respect that we all have our own values and beliefs and these are personal to us.

We feel that if a doll is provided to a person which offers them comfort, reassurance and stimulation then we really need to justify why we would deny a person of these feelings?

It is vital, therefore, that the therapeutic value of doll therapy is fully described to those who are living with or supporting the person with a Dementia.

There have been many studies into doll therapy over the years, e.g. Mackenzie et al and James et al (both 2006). Both carried out research which focused on the impact of introducing dolls and, amongst other things, whether there were any improvements to the residents' activity levels and feelings of anxiety.

Mackenzie stated that around 93 per cent of staff believed there to be a positive impact. James et al also identified benefits to well-being and also a preference towards the doll as opposed to any other 'objects of reassurance' such as teddies or blankets.

What can be done?

- Consider purchasing a professional doll that is designed specifically for Dementia. Please be aware that, whatever supplier you chose, the doll should not cry as this can upset the person if they are unable to control the crying.

- When the doll is introduced, allow plenty of time and either place the doll in chair or crib near to the person or, alternatively, sit quietly with the doll and take the lead from the other person as to whether they show any interest or not. This way, we are not 'forcing' the doll on others.

- Don't label the doll a 'doll' or give it a name! Wait until the person has accepted the doll and takes the lead to provide a name (or not).

- If accepted, offer a 'Moses basket' or crib for the doll to sleep in. Again, see if this is accepted or not or whether the person prefers to use a different place.

- Ensure that the person's behaviour is discreetly monitored to establish if they are getting tired or irritated with the doll so that you can offer to remove the doll or help them put the doll to sleep.

- Consider hygiene and infection control for the doll. In other words, washing the clothes and using bacterial wipes for a bit of a freshen up!

- Once established, document the use of any of this therapy on the PBS plan in the 70 per cent prevention strategies section. This therapy will not be the only strategy used. It is very likely to be part of other meaningful activities and engagement for the person.

3) Pet (or Animal-Assisted) therapy

No matter how unpredictable the day has been, I can count on one absolute constant in my life; when I walk in the door, my sweet Yorkie will greet me as if we've been apart for months. Bad or good days, rain or shine, my little buddy will be beside himself with excitement to welcome me home.

Alzheimers.net

There are numerous studies available that suggest that pets have a positive impact on our well-being, some even suggesting health benefits such as lowering our stress levels, anxiety, blood pressure and boosting our 'feel good' factor. That's got to be good, right?

Personally, I don't need research to tell me this. I just need to walk through the door after spending 4 hours on the motorway and be greeted by my dog, Lily. My Serotonin levels instantly increase and I feel good. In fact, I don't even need to be away from home for any length of time as I get the same welcome from Lily if I have just been in another room to her for 5 minutes!

Having said this, 'pets' are not just cats or dogs. Stimulation can also be gained from listening to bird song by either encouraging birds to feed in the garden or keeping a bird the house (e.g. a budgie). An aquarium of fish can be soothing and relaxing to watch and, for some keeping reptiles, hamsters, rabbits etc. All of these examples serve to promote feelings of love, affection, happiness and a sense of responsibility and purpose to care for the animal.

In Japan, the National Institute of Advanced Industrial Science and Technology have designed a robotic seal as an object of reassurance called 'Paro'. Why a seal? Well, apparently this animal was very carefully chosen. A robotic dog or cat might bring back frightening memories from a bite or barking. Not many people will have unhappy memories of a seal!

The seal, which at the time of writing, cost around $6,000, will make cooing noises similar to baby harp seals and will respond to tone and inflection of the voice. If it is spoken to softly, then it responds with 'gurgles' and turns towards the person. If it detects harshness in the tone, then it will stop what it doing and try something else in order to 'please' the person.

During trials, the seals were found to be particularly helpful around times of 'sundowning' which is towards the end of the day. For some residents, instead of administering medication, the seals were used instead.

Sandra Petersen, a Professor of Nursing at the University of Texas, was supporting a patient with advanced Alzheimers. It was reported that this person had not spoken in eight years. When the seal was introduced to her, the patient cuddled the seal and whispered 'I love you' into its fur.

A far better option than medication I am sure we will all agree!

What can be done?

- The approach and tips for pet therapy will be very similar to that of doll therapy in that you would need to gather information on whether the person (or others around) even likes animals.

- Pets can be either visitors to the home or permanent residents. In every case, the nature and temperament of the pet will need to be risk assessed to ensure that they are able to live happily in the environment. We even know of a residential home that has a pet pony living very happily in the garden!

- Any risk assessment should also include other factors such as whether the pet will jump up to people or has erratic behaviour and potential to cause falls.

- In some instances, where a pet is not an option, a toy animal might be helpful. This could be used for sensory stimulation so that the person is able to stroke the fur, for example.

4) Reminiscence therapy

Reminiscence means the act of remembering past experiences and events.

In general, most people with a Dementia will have a preserved ability to retain their longer-term memory. Reminiscence therapy taps into this strength with a range of tools that help to 'spark' some of these memories.

Research in in Taiwan by Chiang et al (2010) and Woods et al (2009) found that there was a positive effect amongst those people who were involved in reminiscence therapy, citing participants being more sociable, less depressed and showing strong signs of improved cognition and personal well-being. Whilst research is still limited, one considerable finding is that 'no harmful effects were identified' (McKee et al 2003) The Alzheimer's Society also supports the use of reminiscence therapy in their publication Memories are Made of This.

Talking about the past can evoke happy memories and feelings. Having said that, we must remember that the opposite can also be true. This is not necessarily a bad thing but would, of course, need to be treated sensitively. If this is the case, then distraction techniques, moving quickly back to a happier memory, could be used so that the person is not upset for any length of time.

It is also not uncommon for a person with Dementia to repeat the same story over and over again. It could be that the story is a time of their life when they felt particularly proud, happy or sad. This could be reminiscence of their career, friends or family. Listening to the person will help them to feel valued and have a sense of worth.

This, of course, is nothing new. We all like to be listened to if we have something important to share. Of course, we accept and acknowledge that it is not always easy to stay engaged when the story has been repeatedly told! But it is important not to display boredom or disinterest to the person with our body language.

We can, again, use the theory of Maslow's Hierarchy of Needs as a 'checklist' to gather information about the history of the person. The first section of the PBS plan will document all of this information.

What can be done?

There are a range of tools you can use to encourage the person to reminisce:

- We have already covered hints and tips with music, doll and pet therapy which, in themselves can be used to start a conversation and generate memories from the past.

- Life story work can be used. This is a story that is created with staff, family and the person with Dementia to help to review the person's past life. Life story work can be used to reminisce but also to identify what is important to and for the person. Life stories can be generated as books, collages that have images to encourage memory, rummage or memory boxes that have objects that are relevant for the person. This box may include sensory items. Films can be recorded to capture visual information and even messages from family members and the person with Dementia. For earlier stages of Dementia, an 'app' can be used to post memories and events, all of which can be 'liked' or commented on by other users.

- Photographs and images can be used that connect to the person's history. For example, a picture of a shopkeeper or footballer is shown to the person in order to open up imagination and communication. The person can talk about any thoughts or memories that connects them to this photograph.

- When reminiscing, try to avoid 'open' questions. These questions usually start with 'how, why, what, when, where'. Answers to open questions require a lot of processing and can cause an overload, for example 'where were you born'?, 'How many sisters do you have'? 'Closed' questions are preferable, such as 'do you like.....?', 'Have you had.....?' etc

- You can also try reminiscing about your own memories first, not just verbally, but also through images. This may then trigger the thoughts of the person with Dementia and offer them time to start formulating their own thoughts. A closed question could then follow this to see if the person wants to contribute their own memories., e.g. 'did you like…..?'

- We can also tap into all of our senses to trigger memories. We have covered sight, sound and touch. What about smell?. Our sense of smell (through our olfactory bulb) has VIP access to our memory bank (Amygdala and Hippocampus). Don't underestimate this sense – it is very powerful.

- Depending upon the person's communication ability, it may be that actions speak louder than words. Include the person in activities that may trigger their memories. A former landlord of a pub who was tipping other residents out of chairs when they are asleep, shouting 'we are closing now', thinks that the residents who are asleep or slurring words, are drunk! Including this person in daily activities such as clearing the tables away and laying tables and also changing the environment to a pub helped this person reminisce about his life history and, as a result, reduced the behaviours that were causing challenges.

Memory Lane

- Reminiscence work is not just carried out through one to one individual sessions. The work can also be carried out with others by using events such as drama groups, plays, theatre or group sessions. Sessions that everyone can relate to will be a good starting point, covering common subjects such as holidays, school, hobbies or sport.

5) Laughter and play therapy

We all love a good laugh, right? Well, according to research published on Alzheimers.net, laughter, play and being active helps with a range of benefits such as lower stress hormones, ease of anxiety and fear, increase in social interaction and even lower blood sugar levels.

Maybe you have seen the TV series that brings a class of 4-year old children into an older adult residential setting to play and engage in activities with the residents? The results are often staggering: The adults, who may have struggled with mobility or stress and anxiety, become more mobile and happier through play sessions, laughter and the day to day relationships that have developed with the children.

There is also a therapy known as 'laughter yoga'. This is a technique introduced by an Indian physician, Dr. Madan Kataria. This is not like conventional yoga as we know it because, instead, it combines the simulation of laughter with gentle breathing techniques in order to teach the body how to laugh without relaying on humour or jokes.

Dr Kataria believed that the brain cannot distinguish between real and fake laughter and therefore, once triggered, can cause a 'ripple effect'. We can all relate to this, I'm sure. Have you ever heard or seen someone who is crying with laughter – doesn't it put a smile on your face?

Dr Kataria's therapy encourages inducing contagious laughter and, as a result, he states, the yoga sessions improve moods and behaviours for people diagnosed with Dementia. Whilst there is a range of studies published that recognise the benefits of laughter for people with Dementia, at the time of writing, we were unable to find any documented research for laughter yoga (as yet).

In 2017, Pope Lonergan started comedy performances called 'The Care Home Tour' specifically for those diagnosed with Dementia. Lonergan, a part-time stand-up comedian, used to be a full-time carer and stated that he noticed traditional jokes often fell flat with residents. This, he stated, was because people with Dementia can't always follow logic, whereas 'a visual and physical spectacle' (in other words, the 'slapstick' type of humour) has more chance to spark a reaction, even from those residents who were diagnosed with later stages of Dementia.

In summary, we don't really need to read research and studies to conclude that a good chuckle can make us feel good. Having said that, here is some evidence to reflect on: A report, aptly named SMILE, conducted by an Australian research team concluded a very impressive 20% reduction in anxiety following a study of 400 Dementia patients who were simply encouraged to giggle more often! This 20% reduction in anxiety is the same amount as a typical antipsychotic medication!

A further study by Dr. Jean-Paul Bell of Australia's Arts Health Institute tracked the impact of live comedy performances over a 12-week period. The team visited 36 homes in Sydney where they told jokes and played games with the residents. Anecdotally, staff at the homes stated that, during the study, residents were more positive and happier and they had fewer incidents of challenging behaviour reported. The positive effect didn't just stop there – the research stated that the impact continued for up to 26 weeks following the program!

So, what's the message? – laugh more, play more, worry less!

6) Aromatherapy and massage

Aromatherapy comes from two words: aroma (fragrance or smell) and therapy (treatment) and uses essential oils and natural plant extracts in order to promote healing and emotional well-being. There is very little known about the origins of aromatherapy other than credit given to the Egyptians to be first to extract oils from plants and Rene-Maurice Gattesfosse (in 1910) reportedly discovering the virtues of lavender oil.

Aromatherapy can be used in a variety of ways, for example:

- through oil burners or vaporisers
- applied to the skin by massage using a carrier oil
- added to a bath

In terms of research, according to the Alzheimer's Society: *There is some evidence that aromatherapy may be effective in helping people with Dementia to relax, and that certain oils may have the potential to improve cognition in people with Alzheimer's disease. Research has specifically highlighted the potential benefits of the use of lemon balm (Melissa officinalis) to improve cognition and mood in the treatment of Alzheimer's disease, and lavender oil to reduce occurrences of challenging behaviour in Dementia. However, there is currently not enough good evidence to state categorically whether or not aromatherapy is beneficial.*

Dementia.org also states: *Small studies have been conducted into aromatherapy and Dementia. They have shown some encouraging results but more research needs to be done. The main findings of these studies were into the effects of lavender oil, dripped onto a pillow or applied through massage in the form of a cream, and Lemon Melissa balm, rubbed into the skin. Both oils were found to increase the length of time a person with Dementia sleeps for, and decrease signs of agitation such as wandering and excessive movement*

What can be done?

- Before using any oil, especially directly to the skin, medical or professional advice from an aromatherapy expert should be sought. Essential oils may not be suitable for anyone with delicate skin, bruises, allergies or any skin condition or infection.

- As we have already mentioned, smell is very powerful sense. Before any oils are used, try testing the smell out first to see if the person likes it or reacts in any way. We need to ensure that the smell does not trigger any unhappy memories. The oil could firstly be used through a vaporiser in a room or by using a tissue with a drop on it for the person to smell. Do this in a well-ventilated room first.

- Using oils with a calming effect could also be practised at times of 'sundowning' (late afternoon) or towards bedtime.

7) Colour therapy

Professional colour therapy is administered in several ways such as coloured lights, or torch beams, are shone on to the body, different colour liquids are used directly on the body or the person wears different coloured silks. Therapists state that when the range of colour enters our eyes, the light energy of the colour is carried to the centre of the brain. This, in turn affects the body's chakras (centres of energy located in the midline of the body) to stimulate well-being.

Practically, on a day to day basis, we can still use colour therapy in our lives (without the need of formal colour therapy sessions). This might include crystals, gems or jewellery, clothing, flowers or interior colour.

Of course, the feelings we have about colour will be deeply personal and rooted in our own experience or culture. For example, the colour white is usually worn in summer in most Western countries and a symbol of freshness. However, in many Eastern countries white is seen as a symbol of mourning. So, while everyone's perceptions of colour can be different, there are some general consistencies with research into the effects of colour (Margaret Calkins 2002 'How colour throws light on Dementia Care'): Here are some examples:

Yellow: captures the joy of sunshine so is therefore believed to communicate happiness. Yellow is also reported, in colour therapy, to help with memory, mental fatigue and nervousness.

Green: is seen as being connected to peace, calm, growth and nature so, is therefore, deemed as relaxing and refreshing. Green, reportedly, reduces the central nervous system activity which can help people relax. This is why TV studios have 'green rooms' to calm guests before their TV appearance!

Blue is said to bring down blood pressure and slow respiration and heart rate. In 2000, certain areas in Glasgow installed blue street lighting and reported, anecdotally, a reduction in crime. In colour therapy, blue is said to help with communication and soothes tired nerves.

Red is said to raise the heart rate. This could stem from association of red to danger such as fire engines and warning signs. In colour therapy red is stated to aid motivation, passion and strength.

Violet apparently increases artistic and creative abilities. It has been said that DaVinci and Einstein used violet energy for inspiration.

The bottom line is that the effect of colour is a personal thing and may also change depending on how much exposure the person has to it and the different shades of colour. Use this information as a guide only. In other words, we don't have to all dress in green and paint every room in blue in order to promote a relaxed environment!

There is a great deal of research of colour, alongside the contrast and tones of the colour, as being an important environmental consideration for people with Dementia.

What can be done?

- Avoid bold high contrast patterns on floors, especially spots, flecks or stripes as this may cause confusion and disorientation. Stripes, chequered patterns and dark rugs may also be perceived by the person as a step or even a hole in the ground. Stripes and zig-zag patterns can also be perceived as 'moving' objects.

- With floors, avoid using linoleum type floor covering that continues from the floor part way up the wall. This type of covering will make it difficult for the person to recognise where the floor stops and the wall begins. A contrast edge (or border) to a floor covering should also be avoided as this could be perceived as a step. Instead, try to use a continuous plain colour floor covering throughout the building and add a contrast colour for the skirting board. This will help the person distinguish between the floors and walls.

- If there are doors that you need the person to avoid (such as laundry rooms or chemical stores), then try to blend the colour of the door to that of the wall so that the door does not stand out. On the flip side of this, doors that the person needs to access, such as the bathroom or bedroom doors, could have a contrast colour so that it stands out.

- Avoid bold patterns on walls and large flowery or 'swirled' wallpaper. Once again, this can cause confusion to someone with Dementia. We also need to recognise that décor in a residential home needs to suit male and female residents so flowery wallpaper in bedrooms may not feel right for everyone.

- Try to use contrast colours (to that of the floor or wall) for furniture and furnishings such as cushions, chairs, tables, light switches or the toilet seat. This will help the person to see things more easily.

- Use crockery that contrasts with the food and with the table. This also helps with facecloths and towels.

Chapter Eight

Substitute Skills

A substitute skill is an object (or objects) that can be used to provide sensory stimulation. The purpose of this object is to replace a behaviour of concern with a safer option. Let's go through a few examples to show what we mean:

Scenario 1: *Greg has been pulling the hair of people around him and often targets one particular person who is a wheelchair user. When he pulls the hair, he then rubs the hair strands along his face, up his nose and around his ears.*

What's the message? Assessment concluded that Greg is pulling hair for a Sensory function – he get's pleasure from the sensory feel of the hair around his face.

Remember the cogs on page 5?

What's the behaviour? (cog 1): Pulling the hair of others

What's the message? (cog 2): Sensory

What can be done? (cog 3): Introduce a substitute skill:

We tried a variety of substitutes such as fishing wire, hair extensions, fake fur – all of which Greg put to one side. Finally, we introduced a sterile feather. Bingo... Greg immediately started to rub this across his face, pluck the feather and tickle his ears, eyes, nose. He clearly enjoyed this sensory substitute. This was then included in his PBS plan in the 70% prevention section and the feather was placed in his sensory box. Greg stopped pulling hair the day he was given the feather!

Scenario 2: *Kerry is a wheelchair user. When Kerry gets upset or during transition periods (changes in the routine or moving from place to place) she will slap her thigh which causes bruising to her leg (cog 1). Kerry does this for the sensory stimulation of the slapping feeling and sound (cog 2).*

What can be done? (cog 3): Introduce a substitute skill:

Here, we introduced a substitute of a tambourine (with the metal discs removed and a cushion attached) so that Kerry could still experience the feeling of slapping and hear the noise but it stopped the bruising to her leg.

Emily has started to eat (or attempt to eat) objects that are inedible (cog 1). This included smaller objects such as her hearing aid and cotton buds. Emily has also started to consume her own faeces.

Cog 2: What's the message? Tangible

What can be done (cog 3) If you observe someone eating objects that are not suitable for human consumption then this is known as 'Pica'. Pica actually comes from the Latin word of Magpie. This is because Magpies are known to eat anything! Pica would need specialist intervention as there can be many reasons for the behaviour and the risks are high.

Before any strategies are put in place, it might be worth referring the person for iron or nutritional deficiency checks and monitoring bowel movements in order to rule out any medical concerns.

Pica can also occur when the person is unable to recognise the object (Agnosia) and the inappropriateness of what they are doing. In which case, correction or telling the person that 'it is dangerous' or 'it's not good for you' can cause more confusion and upset.

In Emily's case, staff vigilance was key. Smaller, inedible, objects were removed and substituted with edible objects: Raisins, seedless grapes or chocolate buttons, for example.

For stronger tastes, and to substitute the consumption of faeces (known as Scatolia), a range of other substitute items were put in place including items known to contain the chemicals Indole and Skatole (found in human faeces, urine, and saliva and are what gives these substances their strong odour). These (safe) items were certain boiled sweets, candy covered chocolate, synthetic ice cream, stilton cheese and Luwak coffee. All of which are edible substitutes for the consumption of faeces.

In summary, substitute skills would need to be carefully assessed as safe for the person to use and introduced under supervision – just like the use of doll therapy which is also a substitute (for a baby). The substitute object helps the person to meet their need with a less harmful object to replace the behaviour of concern.

Chapter Nine   **70%**

The Alternative to 'No'

For years we have been advising that the word 'no' is generally considered a trigger word. With that in mind, think back over the last month. How many times have you said 'no' to a person you support in response to their request for something? You might not even remember! That is probably because the word 'no' is so easy to say and requires hardly any thought. It is, however, often a knee jerk response. But, we know that 'no' can be a trigger word. So why is this?

We all take denial seriously. Each time you say 'no' to a person you are sending a message that you don't want to help and are refusing the person's request. The word 'no' also evokes a child-like response within us all. Think back to when you were a child. When your parents said 'no', you had four options:

- Ask the other parent hoping you might get a different response

- Ask again, and again, and again (hoping to wear the parent down)

- Accept the response of 'no', but, hey, who wants to do that!

- Cry, kick or scream, hoping that your outburst will change the decision.

You probably thought that you outgrew these responses but, for most of us, these reactions are still evident. We might not kick and scream, but we might 'pout' or sulk. Some common responses to the word 'no' from people we support might be:

- Become agitated and emotional or argumentative to get their viewpoint across

- Go to another person – staff member or others

- Threaten staff or others. Especially if the reason is not understood or there is no other option available to the person.

The alternative to 'no' was initially researched by Duncan Pritchard et al (2014) and we have added a third element to their research (option 3 overleaf). We can now offer three options which can be used on their own or interchangeable:

1. **Yes'** with a **Contingency**

Example: A person wants to buy a bottle of aftershave which is £25 and they only have £15 with them. You could say:

a) No, sorry you haven't got enough money, 👎☹ or

b) Yes. We can go to the bank later to get the extra money and come back to buy it then. 👍☺

2. Offer an 'Alternative Choice'

If the person is asking for something and it is just not available then we can offer the next best option – give the person a choice.

Example: A person wants a hot chocolate drink but the container is empty. You can respond with either:

a) No, sorry we have run out 👎☹, or

b) We haven't got any chocolate but you can have a hot milk or malted drink – you choose. 👍☺

3. Yes with a Consequence

If the person is aware of the risks to and consequences of their actions, you can simply remind them.

Example: If a person is asking for a second (large) bar of chocolate then your response might be:

a) No, you can't have a second bar 👎☹, or

b) Yes, but remember the last time you felt a bit sick when you had too much chocolate 👍☺

We all have a right to make unwise decisions. So, if a person says "I know that a second bar of chocolate might make me feel a bit queasy but it is my choice", then that's OK! We don't always know what the best option is for a person. If they are able to make that choice then why can't they? Even if we personally disagree.

Of course, there is a fourth option........one word: Yes!

In other words, we need to consider why we are saying the word 'no' in the first place. Try conducting a 'no' audit in the workplace. Whenever, you or others say 'no' to a person, look at why this happened. Was it valid? Does this say more about the culture of the home and an underlying concern of a controlling environment?

The Alternative to No can be a powerful tool. Give it a try. It can work in everyday situations!

Finally, remember that with any strategy we use, we will need to adjust our communication to the person strengths and understanding.

Chapter Ten

Defusion and Calming

20%

De-escalation is a strategy that is best used at the early escalation stage – in other words, as soon as possible after the trigger and when the early warning signs present.

The purpose of de-escalation is to take the heat out of the situation and avoid emotions escalating. This needs to start with yourself and an attempt to maintain self-control.

When using de-escalation, we also need to think about how you are coming across to the other person? Particularly think about your non-verbal communication:

- **Facial Expressions** – show that you are listening and attentive. Try to relax your facial muscles and convey openness and empathy with the person.

- **Eye contact** - make appropriate eye contact but avoid constant eye contact that may be perceived as staring – this could be seen as threatening and might trigger aggression.

- **Body Posture** - Avoid aggressive or defensive stances such as arms folded, hands on hips or waving fingers or arms. Try to look relaxed and open.

- **Space** – Consider increasing or reducing space – if appropriate. Remember, when a person starts to get distressed or angry, their personal space may need to be greater than normal and the proximity of others may, at this stage, feel more intimidating (see Chapter 182 Personal Space).

What can be done?

- **Slow down the pace** of your speech – but not too slow as to patronise the person. If we speak slower then it will often have a positive effect on the communication. This, however, may be difficult for us if we are 'in the thick' of a challenging situation (because our Amygdala is reacting now!).

If you can manage to speak slightly slower, however, it will give the other person more time to absorb the information and give you time to think rationally. Remember that the further a person is 'off baseline', then the lower their quality of judgement. Combine this with their diagnosis and there is a real chance that their level of understanding is going to be impaired.

- Keep your voice **steady and calm**, maintain an even tone and pitch, speak gently, clearly and carefully.

- **If the person is shouting** then raise your voice tone to their level – but only initially. If you shout louder than the other person then what are they likely to do? Chances are that they will also increase their voice tone and, before you know it, you are in a shouting match! Once you have matched their level, bring your voice tone down steadily. This has more chance of getting the other person to mirror your voice tone levels.

So, with these general tips in the back of our minds we can then try the **'five steps to de-escalation'**:

Step 1: Identify

Tell the person the name of the emotion. This helps them to understand their feelings and it acknowledges, to the person, that you recognise what they're feeling. However, be sure to correctly identify the person's feeling. If you're not sure, then ask questions. For example, the person might be crying. Rather than saying 'I can see you're angry' (which might elicit a response of 'yes, I am angry' and acting this emotion out) try labelling the emotion as 'you seem very upset'.

Step 2: Actively listen

'If we were supposed to talk more than we listen, we would have two tongues and one ear' (Mark Twain)

'Active listening' means exactly what it says – actively listening. This means that we stop talking, defer judgement and don't jump in with our own advice or comments. This is fully concentrating on what is being said rather than just 'hearing' what has been said. There is a difference.

Various pieces of research suggest that our listening habits are pretty poor. In fact, some researchers state that we only remember between 25% and 50% of what has been said.

Here are some general tips to help develop your active listening skills

- **Show that you are listening.**
  Use your body language to ensure that the other person recognises that you are listening – e.g. nodding your head, 'leaning in' to the other person or even a simple 'uh huh'.

- **Listen for inconsistencies** between the words being said and the behaviour. For example, someone saying they feel calm, but they have gritted teeth and fixed eyes, is showing a very different sign.

- **Avoid distractions**. This can be an external or internal distraction. Noise from the TV, traffic or overhearing others talking are all external distractions. Have you ever tuned into another person's conversation whilst someone is talking to you? Yes? Then you're not listening! Internal distractions can be your own thoughts drifting off to other things like what you need to do next or anything else that jumps in to mind. If you are focusing on this, then, once again, you are not listening!

- In order to better understand what a person is saying to you, try **reflecting back what has been said by 'paraphrasing'** – "So, are you saying that …?"; "Can I just check, do you feel…. is that right?"

- **Resist arguing** - it is very tempting to respond and become engaged in an argument, especially if you are the target of verbal abuse or have been accused in some way. Resist arguing; it is far more likely to result in escalation than help defuse the situation.

Step 3: Empathise

"Empathy can be defined as a person's ability to recognise and share the emotions of another person. It involves, first, seeing someone else's situation from his perspective and, second, sharing his emotions, including, if any, his distress"
Neal Burton 2015

So, empathy means that you are able to relate to the other person's feelings because you have either experienced it or you have the ability to put yourself in the other person's position.

In summary, empathy is different to sympathy. Sympathy essentially **implies** a feeling of **recognition** of other's emotions while empathy is actually **sharing** the emotions, if only briefly.

"The struggle of my life created empathy - I could relate to pain, being abandoned, having people not love me" (Oprah Winfrey)

Step 4: Reassure

Let the person know that you are there to support him/her. Ideally, show the person how to handle the problem on his/her own. This gives a greater sense of accomplishment and self-worth for the person. The person needs to know the problem is under control.

Step 5: Redirect

Try to encourage the person to move (emotionally and physically) in a different direction to a more desired behaviour or activity as soon as possible. Avoid excessive and complex communication when using redirection and don't have more than one person giving directions to an individual simultaneously as this can create an overload of information and lead to confusion.

Chapter Eleven

Planned Ignoring

20%

Planned ignoring simply means to ignore, or not refer to, the behaviour of concern ....but not to ignore the person.

If we react and acknowledge the behaviour of concern (this can even be subtle things like raised eyebrows) then that behaviour has now worked for the person. Remember the old saying 'what we focus on, grows'. Focus on the negative, and that's what you are likely to get. However, if we can redirect the person and focus on positive behaviour then this is what we are more likely to achieve.

Having said this, it is also important to make sure that ignoring the behaviour will not be dangerous or unsafe for the person or others for example hitting others or destroying property. These behaviours cannot be ignored as the risk is too high.

What can be done?

- **Be patient.** "But I tried ignoring and it did not work, in fact, the behaviour got worse!" This can be true. One of the most difficult consequences of planned ignoring is that sometimes the behaviour might increase for a brief time after the intervention begins.

Remember that the behaviour you are ignoring used to 'work' so the person may do more of the behaviour just to test if the response you gave, this time, is a 'one-off'. The secret is to persevere and get others involved too.

- **Pretend the behaviour is not happening.** Unless the behaviour is dangerous, act as if nothing strange is going on and offer no positive or negative reaction. Go about your business as usual but do not ignore the person, just the behaviour. Screaming, what screaming?

- **Use redirection techniques.** Get the person to focus on something else – a more desirable behaviour. For example, if the person is shouting and screaming, ignore the behaviour and re-direct the focus to reinforce a positive behaviour: 'ooh …look at that on the TV'.

- **Leave the area.** You may not be able to control your emotions so, if possible, give yourself some space. You may not be able to do this (due to safety concerns). But, if you can, it can help you ignore the behaviour.

- **Keep a diary** of the behaviour you are ignoring so you can see if it is reducing in frequency. If you have been consistently ignoring a behaviour (that means, not just you, but everyone who is involved with the person) and the behaviour has not been eradicated then there may be another strategy needed.

Chapter Twelve

Reframing skills 20%

Reframing is a strategy that helps us take the 'sting' out of the negative or abusive language in order to attempt to maintain and distract to a positive focus. What we are trying to do is reframe their communication (not the content) by eliminating the harshness of the language. We can achieve this by changing their vocabulary and choosing less provocative and more positive language.

Think about this reframing theory the next time you are standing in in a queue at the supermarket. Some checkout operatives may say something along the lines of "Sorry to keep you waiting". This is giving an apology and has negative connotations.

Most supermarkets have now trained their staff to reframe this to "thank you for waiting". This statement assumes a more positive approach of thanking you and is, in turn, more likely to get a positive response from you (even if inside you are seething at the delay). Remember, behaviour breeds behaviour. Their positive behaviour is more likely to breed your positive behaviour!

Try this exercise to reframe some of the examples:

Original sentence	Give an example of a reframe	Handy hint
"My drink is half empty."		Think of the opposite angle
"I'm stupid and always get things wrong. I never get anything right. I only got 4 out of 10 answers correct in the quiz		Concentrate on any positive aspects.
"She's an idiot. I don't trust her. She's taken my money"		De-personalise and get to the root of the concern.
"I hate that person next door. He is always annoying me with his rubbish music."		De-personalise again and offer a solution.

Refer to page 199 for some suggested answers

Chapter Thirteen

Personal Space

10%

Generally speaking we like to keep our distance from people we don't know very well. Think about it. What do you do in a crowded lift? Look away, look at the floor – basically anything to avoid eye contact. There is a message to why you are doing this. What do you think that is? Escape or avoidance perhaps?

We do this all the time. If you were sitting on an empty bus and the next person to get on then sits next to you, how would you feel? Chances are you would feel a bit anxious or even angry that they didn't chose an empty seat elsewhere. That's why most people would put their bags on the chair next to them – to stop anyone sitting in their personal space.

We also generally prefer to avoid direct eye-to-eye positions as it can feel confrontational – like the two cats hissing and squaring up to each other on a wall. Have you ever had a door-to-door salesman visit your house? They knock on the door and, when you open it (if they have been trained), they will turn to the side. They do this because it gives the other person more open space and then they might say *'not trying to sell you anything'* (yeah right!).

When working closely with someone, hoisting or personal care, try to sit or stand at a slight angle as this will feel less confrontational.

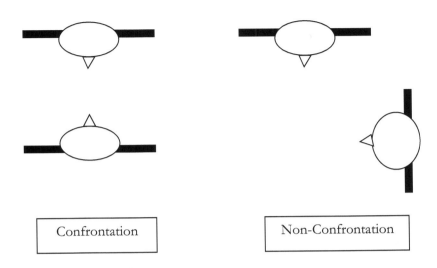

| Confrontation | Non-Confrontation |

For example, if you are a worker who does home visits, then we are not asking you to go into someone's lounge or kitchen and start re-arranging the furniture – this could very easily lead to challenging behaviour! Just turn your body slightly, if you can, during the conversation.

Positions where another person is towering over you can also feel uncomfortable – imagine how this would feel if you are a wheelchair user. Try to bend, crouch down or sit, if possible, when talking to another person who is in a seated position.

There are very specific social rules about how close we can go towards others in particular situations. This *social distance* is also known as *body space* and *comfort zone*. Some people need help to understand these zones as they may not have the spatial awareness to recognise when they are in somebody else's personal zone.

Some people are more comfortable than others with close personal space. You can notice this by watching people's reactions – their early warning signs. If you feel safe and they seem not to feel safe (as they are showing signs such as turning their head, looking away or even laughing with embarrassment) then maybe you need to back away a bit.

So, what are the Personal Space Zones?

Different countries have different 'rules' about social zones. The overcrowded nature of some Asian countries means that they are generally more accustomed to talking to others at a very close distance. Watch a Japanese person talking, in a social situation, with a European person. The Japanese person will step in and the Westerner will usually step back.

The following 'zones' are guidance on general personal space in most western cultures:

Public Zone: Over 12 feet (4 metres+). This is the ideal space required in public situations. In general, we will try to keep at least this distance from people if we are walking around outside. There are, of course, many times when we simply cannot do this. In a market, for example. The theory of the public zone tells us that we will start to notice other people who are within this radius. The closer they get, the more we become aware and ready ourselves for appropriate action, possibly flight or fight.

Social Zone: 4 - 12 feet (1.5m - 4m). This zone is reserved for newly formed groups and acquaintances. Acquaintances are people you know and recognise, but do not have a close relationship with, for example, a neighbour, work colleague or someone you don't see very often.

Personal Zone: 1.5 feet to 4 feet: This is about an arm's length and a half away from the other person which is generally our comfort zone with friends or family or when shaking hands with someone.

Intimate Zone: Less than 1.5 feet: This zone is reserved for people who are emotionally close to us – lovers, parents, siblings, very close friends and pets! It often occurs during intimate contact such as hugging, whispering or touching. Entering the Intimate Zone of somebody you don't know very well can feel threatening and uncomfortable for the other person.

Let's just reflect on this for a moment. How many times do you enter the Intimate Zone when supporting someone with general day-to-day activities? You are in their 'up close and personal space' and definitely in the Intimate Zone when carrying out tasks such as personal care, for example:

- washing, bathing, showering

- shaving

- oral hygiene and denture care

- hair care

- nail care, including chiropody and podiatry

- using the toilet and continence needs

- dressing and undressing

If you need to do any of these tasks then remember that, for most people, maintaining personal hygiene is a very private activity. If the personal care is continually 'forced' and becomes a struggle then you need to think about What can be done? to make it a better experience for you, as a carer but, more importantly, for the person receiving the care. Forced care is likely to have a long-lasting negative impact on the person and, potentially, lead to challenging behaviour.

When helping someone with personal care, be sensitive and, at all times, help the person to maintain their dignity. To make the activity as pleasant and comfortable as possible:

What can we do?

- Use pleasant-smelling shampoo, bubble bath or soap

- Play relaxing music that the person likes

- Try using distraction techniques or give objects of reassurance to refocus the person

- If the person is confused, explain what's happening as you go along

- Try to choose the best time of day for the person and keep to a routine

- Be sensitive to the mood of the person

- Don't make assumptions about appropriate standards of the person's hygiene. What you think is an appropriate amount of time to go without a shower or a bath may be completely different to what the person wants.

- Get the person to help. Ask them to focus on an area of their body and demonstrate what they can do. For example, use a flannel and show the person to rub their arm or leg with the flannel.

- Observe for early warning signs – do they look upset or embarrassed? If so, maybe postpone the session to a different time. What is more important at that time? Having the shave or shower or not being embarrassed or upset?

Chapter Fourteen

10%

Emergency Support and Debrief

The period of time following an incident or crisis needs to be handled sensitively. Emotions will still be high so any discussion about the event will need to wait until the person has returned to baseline. Remember that, before the person actually returns to a baseline stage, they may go through a period of feeling remorseful or tired and may need to spend time on their own to reflect or recover.

It is also important to remember not to place any demands on a person until they have fully recovered. This could be as simple as asking the person to apologise. It may be that the person requires hours or even days to consider this. It will be very much dependent upon the severity of the incident and the personality of the person involved.

At emergency or crisis point, support should also be on hand for everyone else who experienced the event. This includes the person themselves, onlookers and staff.

Those involved in the management of the incident should also conduct what is known as a 'debrief' of events. This should occur as soon as possible after an incident and gives everyone the chance to express their feelings. It does not involve apportioning blame or reprimand. It is about learning, so there should be an attempt to discover the facts regarding the situation and begin to look at how the incident was managed during the crisis and how things might be handled differently, or better in the future.

Here are some suggested questions to consider for a debrief session:

- How does the person feel about the event?
- How do other people feel about the event?
- How does the staff member feel about the event?

- What was good about how the situation was dealt with?
- Is there anything else that could have been done to manage the situation better?
- How can we improve our response?
- Could it have been prevented?
- What changes need to be made to the individuals support plan?
- Does there need to be any additional support for staff, the person or others?

As we are now drawing to the end of this book, we would now like to reflect back to the start and share with you what happened with Derek ....

Chapter Fifteen

And finally . . .

So how did the story end with Derek?

Derek was a mechanic in the army. He also loved the great outdoors. He was known to walk miles and was 'happiest in the hills'.

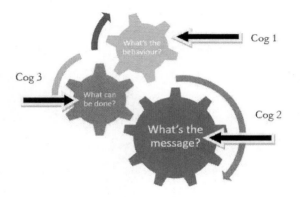

Cog 1: What's the behaviour? You'll recall that Derek's behaviours included:

- Entering other resident's bedroom
- Shouting at staff and other residents
- Climbing on window ledges and rattling doors and window latches
- Hitting staff or anyone attempting to intervene

Cog 2: What's the Message? Escape or Avoidance: The window ledges that Derek would stand on had views over the open fields, sheep, sky, sunset, sunrise… all of which he loved. The desire for wide open spaces had not left Derek.

Cog 2: Tangible: His need to dismantle things within the home was from his life history. This is what he did for all of his career. The need to have a sense of purpose had not left Derek.

Cog 3: What can be done?

- **The seating arrangements** were changed. Instead of having all of the lounge chairs facing inwards (in a horseshoe style), turn some chairs to face outwards – looking out of the window. This will ensure that Derek is able to choose a seat that has a view from the main window. Derek also prefers to sit alone in the lounge or communal areas so Derek now has a chair which has a table next to it. Derek's bedroom also has a chair that faces side on for an internal and external view.

- Derek now has a 'rummage' box. This is filled with objects that he can use to dismantle and put back together.

- Derek has some old Haynes manuals and a range of different pictures and collages to help him reminisce.

- Derek has a plot in the garden that he tends (with additional support).

- He goes for walks, with staff, around the local area and nearby boating lake.

- Colour was used and one of the walls in his bedroom was painted pale blue (with white clouds)
  .

- To help Derek recognise his bedroom, he now has a picture of himself in the army on the door along with a picture of his favourite mountain – Cader Idris in Wales.

- Staff are more understanding of Derek's needs and background so don't try to move him away from the windows now. However, if Derek goes to stand on the window ledges, staff use planned ignoring (they avoid saying 'don't stand on the ledge Derek') and then distraction techniques by asking Derek to talk about walking in the country or his life as a mechanic.

Sometimes, the simplest of changes can make the biggest impact. Derek no longer stands uses challenging behaviour to get his needs met.

What's the message?

Answers to exercise:

Behaviour description from Page 20

Drunk	Throws objects at staff
Slams doors	Aggression
Hits leg causing bruising	Physical
Repetitive questions about home	Makes sexist comments to others
Threatening	Gets angry
Emotional	Anxious
Screams and shouts at others	Frustrated
Shouts at own reflection in glass or mirror	Verbal

All the shaded boxes are clear descriptions or behaviour.

Frustration, anxiety, anger, emotional are all emotions. These emotions may be the 'trigger' to challenging behaviour but are not the behaviour.

Similarly, being drunk is not a behaviour. It may be the 'cause' of challenging behaviour, for example, slamming doors or throwing objects at staff, but it is not a description of behaviour in itself.

Finally, verbal, threatening, aggression and physical are simply to vague and does not offer us a clear enough description of what the challenging behaviour looks or feels like.

Answers to exercise:

The Crisis Cycle from page 37

You are supporting a person who has just punched a relative and shouted 'all of you, go away'. He has now left the room in the direction of his bedroom. What would you do?

---

a) Follow him and ask him to come back and say sorry to the other person and discuss what happened

b) Leave him alone.

c) Go to check he is OK from a distance, check the other person is OK and, when satisfied all is well, monitor from a distance.

d) Go to check he is OK and attempt to calm the situation.

The correct answer would ideally be c). Asking someone to apologise or placing any demands at a Crisis Stage will just put more pressure on the person. This could then re-trigger events and emotions. Wherever possible, we should monitor the person but give them time to return to a baseline state so that their quality of judgement can return.

Next:

Would it be best to:

a) Speak to the person immediately while the incident is fresh in their mind?

b) Wait for about 30 minutes and then discuss it?

c) Wait for about 90 minutes and then discuss it

d) Don't discuss it. The situation has happened and so it is best to just leave it.

The correct answer is c). Maybe b) if the person has not gone to full crisis and has, therefore, returned to Baseline quickly.

Answers to exercise:

The Human Brain from page 61

a) Right

b) Left

c) Left

d) Left

e) Right

f) Right

g) Left

Which Lobe? from page 72

a) Temporal and Occipital

b) Occipital

c) Frontal

d) Temporal

e) Occipital

f) Frontal

g) Temporal

h) Frontal

i) Frontal

Answers to exercise:

Face Blindness from page 129

Philip Schofield

Michael McIntyre

Kate Middleton

Sandy Toksvig

Wayne Sleep

Theresa May

Answer to exercise. Reframing page 181

Original sentence	Give an example of a reframe	Handy hint
"My drink is half empty."	My drink is half full!	Think of the opposite angle
"I'm stupid and always get things wrong. I never get anything right. I only got 4 out of 10 answers correct in the quiz	That's 4 that you got right – that's a good score	Concentrate on any positive aspects.
"She's an idiot. I don't trust her. She's taken my money"	When or where did you last see your money? Let's sort this out and see if we can find it	De-personalise and get to the root of the concern.
"I hate that person next door. He is always annoying me with his rubbish music."	Is it the music too loud or is the type of music that you don't like? Shall we ask him to turn it down or play it at certain times of the day?	De-personalise again and offer a solution.

Answers to exercise:

Personal and Environmental Conditions – from Page 93

Personal	Environmental
Jealous	Hot/Cold
Bored	Crowded
Can't cope with crowds and noise	Noisy
Hungry/Thirsty	Bright or dull colour
Does not like being rushed	Chaotic or unstructured
Tired	Quiet
Excited	Controlling
Medication review	Over stimulating
Need toilet	Unfamiliar surroundings
Depressed	Challenging
Lonely	Untidy
Frustrated	Smelly
In pain, discomfort	Too dark or too light
Angry	Change of routine

Glossary of Terms

ABC chart: Antecedent, Behaviour and Consequence. A behaviour recording chart used within Positive Behaviour Support planning.

Agnosia: Inability to recognise objects

Alzheimer's Disease: Alzheimer's disease is the most common form of Dementia (around 60 to 80 per cent of diagnoses). Alzheimer's Disease is thought to be caused by abnormal amounts of proteins in the brain that interfere with and damage nerve cells and is generally considered to be rare for under-65s.

Aphasia: is an impairment of language, affecting the production or comprehension of speech and the ability to read or write

Apraxia: difficulty with the motor planning to perform tasks or movements when asked

Challenging behaviour: 'Culturally abnormal behaviour(s) of such an intensity, frequency or duration that the physical safety of the person or others is likely to be placed in serious jeopardy, or behaviour which is likely to seriously limit use of, or result in the person being denied access to, ordinary community facilities. Eric Emerson 1995

Creutzfeldt-Jakob disease (CJD) According to the Alzheimer's Association, CJD is one of the rarest forms of Dementia with only 1 in 1 million people being diagnosed with it every year. CJD progresses very quickly, and people often die within a year of diagnosis.

Dementia: Dementia is the umbrella term used to describe a number of different conditions which affect the brain

Echolalia: repetition of another person's spoken words

Frontotemporal Dementia: is considered to be the second most common form of dementia for under-65s. It is caused by damage to cells and pathways in the Frontal and Temporal Lobes of the brain

Lewis Bodies: is a type of Dementia that shares symptoms with Alzheimer's disease and Parkinson's disease so, because of this, can often be misdiagnosed. LB accounts for around 4% of Dementia overall. LB can affect those under and over 65.

Mixed Dementia: is a term used when a person is diagnosed with more than one type of Dementia.

Neurotypical: is a term used to describe typical developmental, intellectual and cognitive abilities in the brain

Object of reassurance: A object used as a comforter, e.g. doll, cuddly toy, or more obscure objects can even be bottle tops etc

Object of reference: an object used to communicate, for example, a cup to indicate a cup of tea or drink, a razor to indicate a shave

PICA: is a psychological disorder characterized by a person eating non-edible food stuffs. This could be faeces, chalk, metal, paint, glass etc.

Positive Behaviour Support: is a behaviour management system used to understand what maintains an individual's challenging behaviour

Posterior Cortical Atrophy (PCA) was first described in 1902, by the neurologist Arnold Pick. PCA is not a common Dementia and is similar in symptoms to that of Alzheimer's Disease. PCA is estimated to be present in about one in every twenty people diagnosed with Dementia

Proactive strategies: Interventions used to prevent trigger events and meet the needs of the person

Prosopagnosia: the inability to recognise faces

Vascular Dementia: is considered to be the second most common form of dementia in the over-65 age group. Vascular Dementia is caused by blood circulation problems (including clots, burst vessels or blocked arteries) within the brain.

Working memory: Part of the brain that processes sequential memory

Young-onset Dementia: is a term used if a person is diagnosed with Dementia before the age of 65. The age of 65 has been used because it is the time when, generally, people have retired from work. That is the only reason and is nothing to do with any biological reasons.

Acknowledgements

We will keep this brief and proportionate to the size of the book.

Thanks to all the staff, carers and patients that we've worked with over the years - both personally on a one-to-one basis or through our training courses. The idea for this book was inspired by these people.

Thank you, as always, to Jill Carnall for the photography and book cover design. Also to Julian Haywood for his overall support with structuring and proof-reading the book – any typos – blame him! ☺

Thanks go to James and Amy Stewart for agreeing to have their pictures published in the self-awareness exercise – especially as these were taken in their early teens!

Final thanks go to our team of instructors spread 'the Message' across the length and breadth of the UK.

www.whatsthemessage.co.uk

References

Alzheimers Society

Eric Emerson (1995): *Challenging Behaviour: Analysis and Intervention in People with Severe Learning Disabilities.* Cambridge University Press

Hodgson LA (1998) *Visual Strategies for Improving Communication. Practical Supports for School and Home.* Michigan: Quirk Roberts

Grinder J. and Bandler R. *Neuro Linguistic Programming (NLP)*

Johari Window by Joseph Luft and Harry Ingram

Kaplan and Wheeler, *Assault Cycle,* 1983.

Miltenberger, R. (2008). *Behaviour Modification.* Belmont, CA. Wadsworth Publishing

Phillippa Lally Cancer Research UK Health Behaviour Research Centre based at UCL Epidemiology and Public Health

O'Neill, R., Horner, R., Albin, R., Sprague, J., Storey, K., & Newton, J. (1997). *Functional Assessment and Programme Development for Problem Behaviour: A Practical Handbook.* Pacific Grove, CA. Brooks/Cole Publishing Company

Zarowska E. and Clements J. (1994) *Problem Behaviour and People with Severe Learning Disabilities'* London: Chapman and Hall

17574951R00111

Printed in Great Britain
by Amazon